insight text guide

Anica Boulanger-Mashberg

Twelve Angry Men

Reginald Rose

First published in 2010. Reprinted 2012, 2013, 2015 (twice), 2016, 2017 (twice), 2019, 2020, 2021, 2022 (twice), 2023, 2024.

Insight Publications Pty Ltd
3/350 Charman Road
Cheltenham VIC 3192
Australia
Tel: +61 3 8571 4950
Email: books@insightpublications.com.au

www.insightpublications.com.au

National Library of Australia Cataloguing-in-Publication entry:
Boulanger-Mashberg, Anica.
Reginald Rose's Twelve angry men / by Anica Boulanger-Mashberg.
9781921411694 (pbk.)
Insight text guide.
For secondary school age.
Rose, Reginald. Twelve angry men.
822.914

Other ISBNs:
9781925175301 (digital)

Cover design: The Modern Art Production Group

Printed by Markono Print Media Pte Ltd

contents

CHARACTER MAP

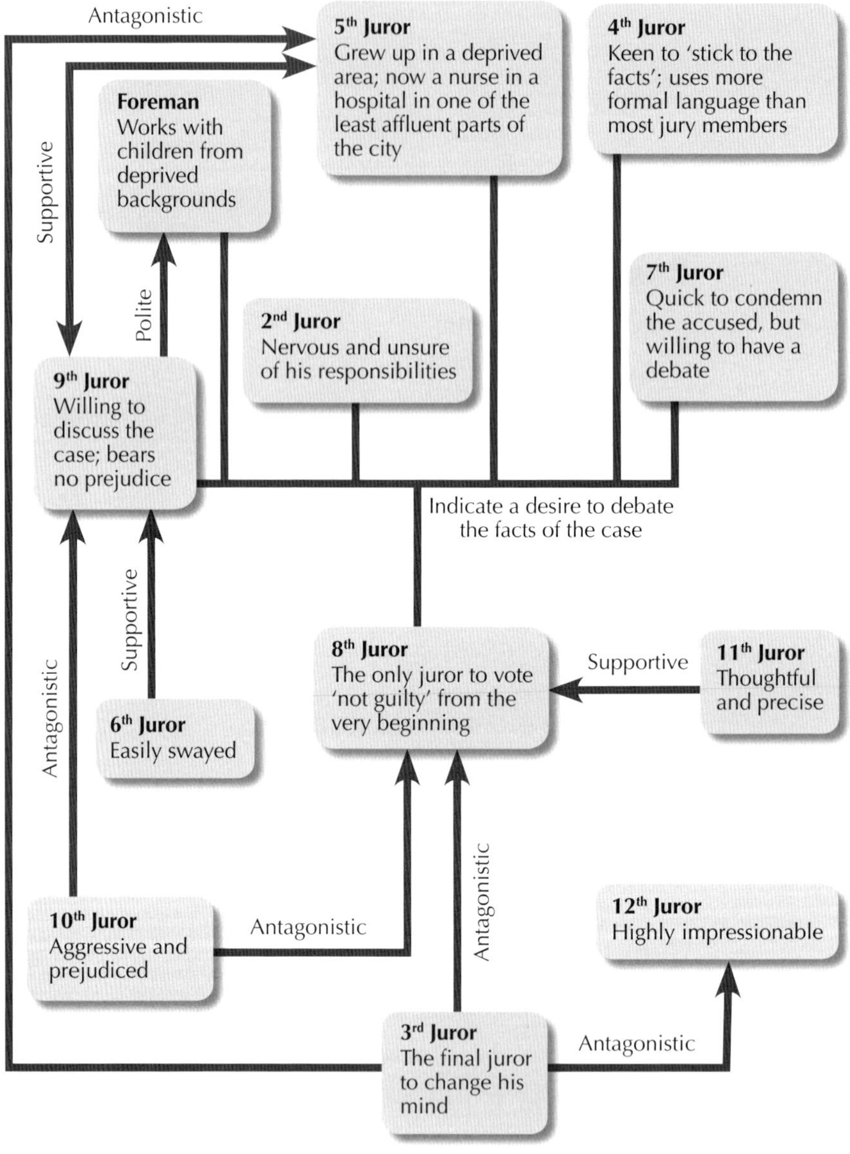

OVERVIEW

About the author

Reginald Rose was born in New York in 1920, and served in the US Army during the early 1940s. He was married twice, and had six children. He began writing for television in the early 1950s, and later worked for all three of America's major television networks. He also wrote for screen and stage, and continued to write, particularly for television, until the late 1990s. Rose died in 2002.

Awards

Among the many recognitions of Rose's contribution to television and screen writing were Academy Award nominations for the film version of *Twelve Angry Men* – which he wrote and co-produced. He also won several Emmy Awards and, for *Twelve Angry Men*, an Edgar Allen Poe Award (Best Motion Picture), and a Writers Guild of America award (screen; Best Written American Drama).

Work

Rose wrote mostly for television, but he also penned several screenplays, including *Crime in the Streets* (1956), *The Wild Geese* (1978) and *The Sea Wolves* (1980). His stage plays include *Black Monday* (1962), *Dear Friends* (1968) and *This Agony, This Triumph* (1972). He had a deep interest in narratives of social justice, and he wrote about social issues he saw around him at the time. He made some controversial choices in his television writing, but at times bowed to pressure from studios to alter scripts so as not to offend or alienate certain audience sectors.

Twelve Angry Men

Although Rose wrote for numerous award-winning television series, and won several Emmy awards for his television writing, he is probably still best known for *Twelve Angry Men*, in all its various forms. He wrote the original teleplay version for the CBS network in 1954, expanded it into the film screenplay three years later, and eventually wrote several stage versions. The revised stage version from the 1970s is the stage script with which we are familiar today.

Rose's inspiration for the play *Twelve Angry Men* came from his own experience as a juror in a manslaughter trial. He was overwhelmed by the process and by the protracted deliberations of the jury, and decided the experience would make a good television drama.

Synopsis

A classic jury-room drama, *Twelve Angry Men* follows a jury's decision-making process in a murder trial, tracking the gradual changing of eleven of the twelve jurors' minds about their verdict.

Twelve Angry Men is set in New York in 1957, and the entire action of the play takes place on one hot afternoon and evening in the jury room of a court of law. The two single-scene acts cover exactly the period of time of the jurors' discussion. The action is continuous with no change of location, which contributes to the play's overwhelming sense of emotional tension and claustrophobia.

The twelve angry men of the title are the twelve men of the jury. They are identified in the script only by jury numbers (and Foreman), and there is no evidence that they even know each other's names. This is indicative of the play's focus on the case and its broader ethical implications, rather than personal details of individual characters' lives. When details do emerge, they are only ever discussed with reference to their influence on the particular juror's vote. The only other character who appears in the play is a guard who serves only a perfunctory and practical purpose in the text. Similarly, the defendant, victim, lawyers and witnesses in the trial are never named.

The play begins at the conclusion of the court's exploration of the case, when the jury must retire to the jury room and decide on a verdict. The opening lines are the Judge's offstage voiceover, reminding the jury of their duty and at the same time furnishing the audience with the basic details of the trial – including the important fact that the jury must reach a unanimous verdict.

We are introduced to the bare facts of the case (further details of the case emerge gradually), as the jury agree to a preliminary and informal vote. Eleven of the twelve jurors are convinced that the defendant, a young boy from an underprivileged socio-economic background, is guilty of fatally stabbing his father.

In this first vote, 8th Juror stands alone. He maintains that he is uncertain and therefore *must* vote 'not guilty'. This decision introduces an important legal concept to be examined over the course of the play: for the jury to convict the accused, they must be confident, *beyond reasonable doubt*, that the defendant is guilty. While 8th Juror does not yet suggest that the defendant is innocent, he feels that there *is* reasonable doubt about whether the boy really committed the crime, and is therefore compelled to vote 'not guilty'.

As the play progresses, jurors regularly call for informal votes (both secret and public) to see where opinion stands. With each vote, jurors become less certain, swayed by arguments and questions presented first by 8th Juror and later by others too. By the end of the first act, after three votes, two jurors have changed their minds so that the vote stands at 9:3, still in favour of convicting the defendant. 8th Juror is gently persuasive in the face of anger, frustration, criticism and challenge from other jurors – particularly 3rd and 10th. The tension and conflict increase as jurors begin to question their own beliefs and change their votes.

Details of the trial emerge in the course of the deliberations, helping us understand the jurors' 'guilty' votes. But as witnesses and witness statements are questioned, the audience, like the jurors, finds itself increasingly open to doubt. For example, in the first act 8th Juror produces a switch-knife identical to the one presented as evidence in court. The prosecutors had argued convincingly for the uniqueness of this particular weapon, but 8th Juror's ability to produce an identical weapon erodes the others' confidence that the evidence proves the defendant's guilt *beyond reasonable doubt*.

To change their votes to 'not guilty', 8th Juror must only introduce reasonable doubt into the other jurors' deliberations; he need not demonstrate the defendant's innocence. This makes his task easier, and he proceeds to provoke doubt amongst his fellow jurors, slowly and patiently questioning a series of arguments, statements and pieces of evidence from the trial. Several other jurors also begin to question these previously accepted 'facts' until, near the end of the second act, eight jurors have changed their vote and now only three (3rd, 4th, and 10th) remain convinced of the defendant's guilt.

At the height of the conflict, 10th, 4th and finally 3rd jurors change their minds. The denouement of the play is swift and tidy as the jurors reach a unanimous verdict of 'not guilty', before making their exit to deliver their verdict to the court.

Character summaries

Guard: A minor character; the guard enters several times to deliver exhibits from the case at the jury's request.

Foreman: The Foreman of the jury, or principal juror, is in charge of running the proceedings in the jury-room. Although he is ultimately responsible for delivering the verdict, he has no more power than the others. Nor does he assert his position or appear more confident than anyone else; he simply fulfils his role of coordinating the group. He is the seventh juror to change his vote to 'not guilty'. We learn that the Foreman is a football coach at a high school in Queens.

2nd Juror: A first-time juror, he is slightly nervous and anxious about the proceedings and about his responsibilities. He is the equal-fourth juror (along with 6th) to change his vote.

3rd Juror: 3rd Juror is married and has a twenty-year-old son with whom he has a troubled relationship. He runs a messenger service. Confident and sometimes aggressive, 3rd Juror describes himself (perhaps sarcastically, but seemingly accurately) as 'the competitive type' (p.54). He has been a juror before and thinks this case is clear-cut. He is resistant to 8th Juror's arguments and is the final juror to change his vote.

4th Juror: The ninth (second-last) juror to change his vote. We learn that 4th Juror is a broker.

5th Juror: A fan of the Milwaukee baseball team, 5th Juror grew up in a slum environment. He works as a nurse in Harlem Hospital (a hospital in a poor area). He is the second juror to change his vote.

6th Juror: A house painter, he is the equal-fourth juror (along with 2nd) to change his vote.

7th Juror: A fan of the Yankees baseball team, he is the fifth juror to change his vote.

8th Juror: The only juror to vote 'not guilty' at the first vote. An architect with two children, 8th Juror is generally calm, reasoned and rational. He stands by his position and eventually persuades all the other jurors to vote 'not guilty'.

9th Juror: An older man and the first juror to change his vote.

10th Juror: 10th Juror runs garages for a living. Confident and assertive, he is the eighth juror to change his vote.

11th Juror: A watch-maker of German background, he is the third juror to change his vote.

12th Juror: 12th Juror works for an advertising agency and this is probably not his first experience on a jury. He is the sixth juror to change his vote. He changes his vote twice more: back to 'guilty' (p.54), and finally to 'not guilty' (p.57) near the conclusion of the play. He is the only juror to change his vote more than once.

Offstage characters regularly discussed

The defendant: A sixteen-year-old boy accused of fatally stabbing his father. He comes from an underprivileged socio-economic background and has a history of abuse by his father. He has a prior criminal record, including theft and violence, and has appeared in a Children's Court and served time in a Reform School. The defendant may be a member of a racial minority but this is only ever hinted at.

The victim: The defendant's (deceased) father. He had a history of gambling, violence, unstable employment and had been in prison. He is described as not 'exactly a model citizen' (p.23).

In the court room: The jury regularly discuss characters who were present in the court room, including:

- the *prosecuting attorney* for the case
- the *defence counsel* for the case
- the *first witness* (as referred to in the jury room): an old man living in the apartment below the defendant and victim
- the *second witness*: a woman living across the street; she could see from her window into the defendant/victim's apartment
- further *witnesses*: neighbours from across the hall.

BACKGROUND & CONTEXT

Social and historical context

Twelve Angry Men paints a portrait of a small portion of American society in the mid-1950s. Worldwide, economies had recovered from the Great Depression of the late 1920s and 1930s, and America had emerged victorious and strong from the second World War. The challenges facing American society were no longer to do with basic survival, but instead about negotiating America's place in a global political environment. America was engaged in an ongoing conflict with the Soviet Union (the Cold War) which continued for many decades. This was a struggle for political and economic dominance between two very powerful nations, and was not always military, but often social, political and economic. At the same time, the nation was entering into an internal struggle, the Civil Rights Movement, which was concerned with ending racial discrimination and promoting freedom, respect and equality.

Rose's play presents a situation of domestic conflict which echoes this backdrop of social and political conflict in 1950s America. In *Twelve Angry Men*, not only are there clashes of individual personality and belief, but there are glimpses of the class conflicts and philosophical challenges facing working-class Americans. An exploration of the legal system, Rose's play does not so much critique as attempt to humanise the American constitutional judicial process for audiences.

Publication and production history

Rose's 1977 version of *Twelve Angry Men* is a revised edition of his original stage play, itself a version of both the screenplay and the original television script. The work has survived rewrites and shifts from one medium to another, and has also been adapted by other writers, including as *Twelve Angry Women* or *Twelve Angry Jurors* (for female or mixed-gender casts); in translation for both stage and screen, and even in an Indian Bollywood remake. Rose is also credited as the writer of the 1997 American telemovie version.

The 1957 film version was co-produced by Rose and Henry Fonda, the actor who played 8th Juror. Fonda had enjoyed the telemovie and was keen to see a film version made, but it wasn't easy to get studios interested in the project. Rose and Fonda financed the film themselves, and although it remained one of Fonda's favourite films and was nominated for an Academy Award, it was never a commercial success. Despite this, it has won critical acclaim and is now recognised as a classic of American cinema. The stage version is also still regularly produced and adapted.

(Further discussion of the 1957 film version and the 1997 telemovie can be found in the 'Different Interpretations' section of this guide.)

Legal context

Twelve Angry Men is a legal drama, and as such requires knowledge of some legal terminology and a basic familiarity with the twentieth-century American judicial system. However, Rose's intention was never to create a play which could only be appreciated by those with a detailed legal understanding. On the contrary, the play is about the very human challenges of jury duty, and how this illuminates human judgement and decision-making processes.

Legal jargon in the play is kept to a minimum; where specific concepts are explored, they are always discussed between characters so that audience members are not alienated. For example, the central notion of 'reasonable doubt' is discussed in depth so that characters (and audience) may come to terms with the concept. 8th Juror explains: 'we're supposed to decide whether or not the boy on trial is guilty beyond a reasonable doubt' (p.23) and later notes that there are so many 'maybes' about some of the evidence, that 'there's enough doubt to make us wonder' (p.30).

Theatrical context

The 1950s was a decade responsible for many classics of American theatre. The thriving Broadway cultural scene signified the importance of theatre in New York's cultural environment. As a writer for the stage, Rose's contemporaries included Tennessee Williams and Arthur Miller, and while *Twelve Angry Men* is considered a classic of American drama, Rose himself never achieved the respect or renown of dramatists like Williams and Miller (perhaps in part because television was his main medium, more so than the stage). Histories of American drama rarely acknowledge Rose or his works.

Rose's stage work sits comfortably within the category of post-war mainstream American drama, which is described as being 'middle class in subject and attitude, realistic in intent' (Downer 1961, p.19). While European drama was venturing into theatre of the absurd, the American theatre was instead concerned with 'psychological veracity' and the experience of social conflict (Bigsby 1992, p.127).

GENRE, STRUCTURE & LANGUAGE

Genre

Twelve Angry Men is a ***drama***: a serious rather than comedic play. It is not 'serious' in the way of tragedy, and therefore not constrained by the formal or structural requirements of a tragedy. It employs the style and techniques of realism and naturalism.

Naturalism and realism

Naturalism in theatre emerged in the late-nineteenth century and is a specific theatrical style building upon the traditions of realism – a movement taking place at around the same time. Both 'naturalism' and 'realism' are terms frequently used in literary criticism and analysis, and while they sometimes refer to specific movements, they are commonly used as more generic descriptors of style. Both terms refer to theatrical works demanding 'natural' performances (rather than the heightened acting required by other, particularly earlier, theatrical styles), and presenting events and narratives close to 'reality'. Realist or naturalist plays are usually concerned with everyday life. Heightened symbolism, melodrama, and spectacle are never elements of realist or naturalist dramas, which avoid theatrical artifice in their construction and performance. While the two movements are closely related, the distinction between them is that naturalist theatre tends to be more confronting, as it not only refuses to rely on theatrical artifice, but also strives to present real life in all its gritty and mundane detail, even when this is not pleasant or tidy.

The television equivalent of the realist/naturalist style is known as 'slice of life', and Rose's television writing in the early 1950s (including the television version of *Twelve Angry Men*) was at the forefront of this movement.

The stage version of *Twelve Angry Men* embraces realist and naturalist traditions, presenting a gritty everyday legal drama, along with the interpersonal conflicts this generates. Its style is relentlessly realist – the narrative is carried by the concrete action onstage and is rarely emphasised by decorative theatricality or symbolism.

Structure

The play is structured in two acts, commonly divided by an interval. There are no further divisions of action in the script (i.e. no separate scenes), and although characters move in and out of the washroom, and the Guard enters and exits, none of the central characters leave the stage until the play concludes. The lack of scene division or significant change in cast dynamics lends a sense of intensity to the play.

Classical unities

Twelve Angry Men obeys all three classical 'unities' of theatre: the unities of action, place and time. These unities are based on Aristotle's *Poetics*, one of the first philosophical examinations of dramatic and literary theory. Aristotle examined components of drama (specifically tragedy). He articulated some 'first principles' of creative composition and *Poetics*, composed in Greek in the third century BCE, still underlies the ways in which we understand the theatre and literary theory today. Aristotle's arguments suggested that drama must follow a ***unity of action***: there should be only one central plot. *Twelve Angry Men* fulfils this requirement; its single concern is the jury's deliberations and decision. Incidental conflicts between characters and the details of their personal lives all serve this single central plot and do not comprise subplots.

Aristotle never explicitly discussed 'place' but *Poetics* has been understood as arguing that the central action should occur in a single location, and the stage should represent only this location: the ***unity of place***. *Twelve Angry Men* satisfies this criterion.

The ***unity of time*** has similarly been deduced progressively in interpretations of *Poetics*. Aristotle noted that tragedy rarely covered a period longer than a single day. This has been taken as a rule that dramas should occur within a single short period of time, not encompassing significant shifts in chronology (for example, moving backwards and forwards in time).

Twelve Angry Men is a faithful illustration of this unity: the progression of the play is in 'real time', with the time passing on stage equal to the time passing in the theatre. The only exception is the interval, which 'pauses' the stage time. Time is so important in the play that the furniture and props list in the script even mentions the clock that should form part of the set (p.60).

The effect of obeying classical unities

Many of the works we are familiar with in modern English canons do not follow classical unities. Even Shakespeare's plays tend to encompass a multitude of locations and subplots, and sometimes broad passages of time. Certainly twentieth-century theatrical works are not constrained by Aristotle's structural rules, so Rose's choice to follow the unities is a conscious one and not simply the result of convention or expectation.

In *Twelve Angry Men* this allows the audience to feel very close to the characters, their relationships and the conflicts and challenges with which they are faced in deciding the defendant's fate. The unities of action, place, and time create an intense focus on this small portion of these characters' lives, placing the audience in the same kind of enclosed situation that the characters are experiencing. The characters cannot leave the jury-room until their job is done; similarly, we have no escape from their reality until the action of the play concludes. This helps Rose construct the claustrophobic, tense atmosphere of the jury-room. There are no moments of relief or distraction created by scene changes, and all the action takes place before us – the only events collapsed into offstage time and space are those leading up to the trial.

Shape

With no scene breaks to structurally measure out the progression of the play, the movement of *Twelve Angry Men* is instead shaped by content. From early on, we know that a conflict must be resolved, as the decision must be unanimous and not all jurors are in favour of finding the defendant guilty. The progression of the play, then, is shaped by the gradual changing of individual jurors' minds. Votes are regularly taken, and there are clear shifts of opinion in the room as more and more jurors vote 'not guilty'. It is this changing opinion that forms the core of the narrative, shaping the movement of the play.

Q Choose one of the three unities and give an example of how Rose could have altered *Twelve Angry Men* so that it did not obey the unity. How might this change an audience's experience of the play?

Language

In keeping with its realist and naturalist tendencies, the language in *Twelve Angry Men* is very 'natural' – the characters speak with vocabulary and language patterns appropriate to the era and geographical setting of the play.

Style of dialogue

The characters tend to use concrete language rather than heightened imagery, symbolism or metaphor. They are all working-class men unlikely to have the luxuries of high literature, but they do share a social and cultural vernacular of sport, film and even television advertising, and references to these common aspects of their lives (particularly baseball) creep regularly into their conversations in the jury room. When the jurors discuss other possible suspects, 3rd Juror jokes that maybe it was Modjelewski (p.23) – a young baseball player they've already mentioned (pp.4–5).

Legal terminology

As well as sharing a broad social and cultural context, the jurors all share the immediate context of the court case, and they are comfortable with legal concepts. There are a number of specific legal terms in frequent use in *Twelve Angry Men*, and many (such as 'defendant', 'attorney' and 'evidence') will be familiar and do not need definition. Where these terms are less familiar (such as 'reasonable doubt'), they will be highlighted in the scene-by-scene 'key vocabulary' sections the first time they occur in the script.

SCENE-BY-SCENE ANALYSIS

Note: For this guide, the two acts are divided into shorter sections for ease of discussion. These will be called 'units', so as not to confuse them with the standard theatrical term, 'scenes'. Scripts are commonly broken into units during the rehearsal process in order to rehearse small sections within acts or scenes. The division points for units can be subjective, but there are a range of factors that generally dictate the end of one unit and the beginning of the next. These include:

- change in mode (for example, in musicals: a shift from dialogue to dance or song)
- a change in time or location (neither of which are applicable in plays like *Twelve Angry Men*)
- a significant change in emotional tone
- the entrance or exit of a character.

For this guide, I have adopted the following justification for dividing units:

- each new vote within the jury room takes place within its own unit,
- each piece of evidence brought into the room by the Guard determines a new unit, and
- each physical re-enactment or demonstration by 8th Juror also determines a unit.

Unless otherwise explained in unit headings below, units end when a vote is counted, or when the guard exits after delivering an exhibit. Unit numbering continues through to the end of the play rather than starting again for the second act.

Act One, Unit One: First vote (pp.1–7, ends when Foreman '*resumes his seat*')

Summary: *Judge reminds Jury of their task; Guard brings jurors in; jurors vote informally, by show of hands; vote is eleven to one (8th Juror) in favour of guilty.*

We are introduced to the situation as well as the characters, though we don't yet know much about the jurors' personal lives. At this point they are merely defined as members of a jury. This is consistent with the overall tone and focus of the play; we never learn characters' names, and when we do learn details of jurors' or offstage characters' lives, it is always with direct relevance to the case and the immediate conflict in the jury-room.

The Judge's voiceover offers two vital pieces of information that will determine the action and outcome of the play:

- the jury's decision must be unanimous, and

- if there is any 'reasonable doubt' about whether the defendant committed the crime, then the jury's verdict must be 'not guilty'.

Key point

The notion of 'reasonable doubt' underlies much of the Western contemporary justice system in countries including America and Australia, yet the term is notoriously difficult to define because it is not absolute: it is possible for a juror to have *some* doubt about the defendant's guilt without it constituting what is legally known as *reasonable* doubt.

This first unit establishes the oppressive New York summer heat, reminding us how claustrophobic the room must feel physically, and at the same time foreshadowing the emotional and psychological 'heat' and conflict to come.

Although the conversation is general, some important details are revealed. For example, 3rd Juror, while stating his support for the moral right to a fair trial, reveals prejudices: 'sometimes I think we'd be better off if we took these tough kids and slapped 'em down before they make trouble, you know? Save us a lot of time and money' (p.3). He feels the verdict is a foregone conclusion, and is keen to finalise a verdict. 7th and 10th Jurors are similarly confident that the decision will be made quickly (p.4). 10th Juror, like 3rd, casually reveals some of his own prejudices, including judgements about families from the defendant's social environment and background.

The jury agree to a preliminary vote, with the Foreman reminding them (and the audience) of the mandatory death-penalty for first-degree murder trials. This means if the defendant is found guilty as charged, then the court has no alternative but to sentence the defendant to death – at this time in America, in the electric chair. (In other types of trials, a guilty verdict still leaves courts with a range of options about severity of punishment).

The Foreman also reminds the jurors and audience of the rule of unanimity: the verdict must be 'twelve-to-nothing ... either way' (p.6). The first of the play's six votes is taken – this time by show of hands (pp.6–7). 8th Juror is the only one to vote 'not guilty', and this initiates the play's central conflict. Because of the rule of unanimity, there are only three possible outcomes: that the jury change 8th Juror's mind, that he changes theirs, or a hung jury is declared.

Key vocabulary

Defendant: the person in a court case against whom the legal action is being taken, also commonly known as 'the accused'.
First-degree murder: a murder both premeditated and malicious.
Hung jury: when a jury is unable to resolve differences of opinion to reach a unanimous verdict. As a result the trial is declared a mistrial, and may or may not be retried.
Reasonable doubt: the lack of certainty, based on the evidence presented in the case, of the defendant's guilt. To convict the defendant in a case like this, the jury must be convinced by the prosecution's case, *beyond reasonable doubt*.

Q From this first unit, what can we conclude about 8th Juror's personality?

Q We never learn the characters' names. Why does Rose choose to identify the men only by jury number, and how does this affect the way we relate to the characters?

Act One, Unit Two: First exhibit – the knife (pp.7–15, ends when the guard exits)

Summary: *8th Juror defends his vote; the jurors agree to one hour's discussion, with each to explain their reasons for their vote; 8th Juror requests to see the knife.*

Following the preliminary vote, there is now a clear division in the room, and a conflict to be resolved. Because 8th Juror is in an extreme minority, the other jurors assume that they must change his mind in order to reach a unanimous verdict. Nobody yet imagines that he might change any of *their* minds. 8th Juror does not attempt to convince anyone that the defendant is innocent (this is never really his goal). Rather, his primary argument is that he is simply not convinced of guilt: he has what he will demonstrate to be *reasonable* doubt.

8th Juror's position illustrates both the concept of reasonable doubt and also the underlying Constitutional structure which, as 8th Juror points out, places the 'burden of proof ... on the prosecution' (p.9). It is not necessary for the defence counsel to prove the defendant's innocence, merely to argue – and convince the jury – that his guilt is in question. The prosecution's job is, then, in many ways harder: they must effectively *prove* the defendant's guilt, at least beyond reasonable doubt.

As the jurors present their arguments for voting 'guilty', it quickly becomes clear that personal bias and feelings, combined with a confidently presented case by the prosecution, have led the eleven jury members to a certainty about the defendant's guilt. The reasons they cite for their decisions can be divided into three main categories:

- the personal qualities of the defendant (e.g. character traits, background, age and familial relationships),
- the strength of the prosecution's case and witness statements, and
- the jurors' personal feelings and instincts, probably based on the above, for example, 'it's hard to put into words. I just – think he's guilty. I thought it was obvious from the word go' (p.9).

3rd and 10th Jurors emerge as two of the strongest proponents of the 'guilty' verdict, and also two of the most resistant to calm, reasoned discussion. They're keen to put the case to rest, and their attitudes in this early unit are representative of the remainder of the play: they are the last to change their votes.

The Foreman attempts to bring some form of order to the proceedings, but even his mild attempts to structure the process infuriate 10th Juror. One of the first exchanges of heightened conflict takes place when 5th Juror becomes defensive in response to 10th's generalisations regarding people of poor socio-economic background – a background 5th shares with the defendant (pp.12–13). 10th Juror quickly becomes aggressive, '*his anger rising*' (p.12), and verbally lashes out at the Foreman for trying to smooth over the situation.

Through all of this, 8th Juror remains calm, articulate and unassuming: he is firm about his 'not guilty' vote but he never resorts to aggression, frustration or personal attack in order to make his point. Instead, he reasons through his own response to the case, explaining why he feels unconvinced by the prosecution and why the jury should take some time to discuss the case. He also questions others, challenging their certainty about the verdict. In his explanations, he relies on the same reasons as the others: the defendant's background and character, the strength of the prosecution's case and his own personal feelings.

This unit concludes when the guard exits to fetch the knife, one of the pieces of evidence from the case. Again, 8th Juror demonstrates his willingness to question and to re-question, where other jurors have formed their opinions and are reluctant to re-examine them or have them challenged. For example, when 8th Juror requests to view the knife again, 3rd is impatient, saying 'we all know what it looks like' (p.14).

Key vocabulary

Constitution: The U.S. Constitution, drafted in 1787 (and since amended), establishes the legal and legislative foundation for the country's governance and justice system. Australia's Constitution is a similar legal document upon which all tenets of governance and justice are founded. Neither the American nor the Australian constitutions include the terms 'burden of proof' or 'reasonable doubt', but both countries' judicial systems rely on these principles.

Circumstantial evidence: evidence that is indirect but allows for assumption and inference of a secondary situation, event or detail. (Eyewitness testimony, conversely, is known as 'direct evidence'.)

Q How are we encouraged to sympathise with 8th Juror in this unit?

Act One, Unit Three: Second vote (pp.15–19)

Summary: *Guard delivers the 'unusual' switch-knife; 8th Juror produces an identical knife; jurors discuss the difference between 'possible and 'probable'; 8th Juror calls for another vote; in a secret ballot a second juror votes 'not guilty'.*

The argument now becomes more concrete; this is symbolised by the physical presence of a piece of evidence in the room. The jurors discuss, in detail, their understanding of the knife's role and significance in the case. These kinds of discussions, which occur regularly throughout the play, are a way of letting the audience in on the trial, which took place offstage before the commencement of the play and which the jurors all have in common as shared history. There is minimal exposition in the play: when the audience first meets the jurors, they are familiar with each other and with the case already. The Judge's voiceover is the only concession to the audience's ignorance of the facts of the case. All the details of the case are woven into the ongoing action of the play. For example, 4th Juror's long speech here about the knife's relevance, and the prosecution's basis for relying on it, serves to reiterate information already familiar to the other jurors, while introducing completely new information for the audience (pp.15–16).

At face value, the details regarding the knife seem to be strong evidence against the defendant. However, 8th Juror again questions everyone's assumptions, asking the others to consider the apparently unlikely possibility that the unusual knife in evidence is not unique. Here, we begin to understand the difficulty with the concept of 'reasonable doubt'. What is 'reasonable'? On the face of the evidence presented, 3rd Juror feels convinced, beyond doubt, that the knife is too unusual to have a double, and is therefore indicative of the defendant's guilt. Yet 8th Juror doubts the knife's uniqueness (and, a moment later, reveals why). Which of these men can be considered more 'reasonable' in his beliefs here?

Key point

An interchange between 4th and 8th Jurors reminds us of the difference between 'possible' and 'probable'. 8th Juror, suggesting that someone other than the defendant *could* have killed the victim with the same kind of knife, says 'it's possible'. 4th replies 'but not very probable' (p.17). This reiterates the difficulty of defining 'reasonable' doubt. Not only are interpretations of events subjective, but calculations of probabilities of various alternatives are also subject to great personal bias. What makes one speculation more 'reasonable' than another?

The moment when 8th Juror reveals the second knife is important for several reasons:

- it reveals his strength (as he supports his seemingly idle arguments) and suggests he is a force to be reckoned with and not just someone who will delay the process
- it reveals his fallibility: to acquire the knife he knowingly 'broke the law' (p.17)
- it illustrates the power of tangible 'evidence' in swaying jurors, both in this case and in a general sense: until he reveals the knife, no-one is prepared to entertain his proposal that a similar knife might exist, but after seeing the knife one juror is impressed enough to change his vote.

The jurors now begin discussing the case in earnest, considering the possible implications of the second knife. 8th Juror directly challenges others and questions their opinions, for example, asking 10th Juror about the defendant: 'do you think he lied?', then asking the same question of 4th and 5th jurors (p.18). In doing so, 8th Juror forces the others to publicly confront their assumptions in the face of the new 'fact' he has brought them (the second knife). 5th Juror is the only one to lose any certainty, and it is clear that this admission is not easy for him: he '*breaks off and looks nervously around*' (p.18). Going against the group's strongly held majority opinion is difficult. Perhaps out of sensitivity to 5th Juror's anxiety about his newfound uncertainty, when 8th Juror calls for another vote he suggests that they do so by secret ballot. He adds that he will abstain, and if no-one else changes his vote he agrees to change his own so the deliberations will be over. The rest of the jury consent to vote, and when ballot slips are read aloud by the Foreman, one now says 'not guilty'.

Q Does 8th Juror's revelation of the second knife change your opinion at this stage about the defendant's guilt or innocence?

Act One, Unit Four: Third vote (pp.19–31, ends when Foreman announces the vote is 'eight to four, in favour of "guilty"')

Summary: *Jurors respond aggressively to the outcome of the second vote, accusing 5th Juror of weakness; 9th Juror volunteers that it was he who changed his vote; the knife is returned to the Guard; several Jurors retreat to the wash-room for discussions; 8th Juror questions evidence and witness testimony, then calls for another vote; 11th Juror changes his vote.*

In this unit the discussion regarding the 'facts' of the case begins in earnest, while the conflict and tension in the room continue to escalate. Immediately after the second vote count, 3rd Juror aggressively – and falsely – accuses 5th of being weak and changing his vote. When 9th Juror owns up to having changed his vote, he reiterates 8th's original assertion: the defendant *might* be guilty, indeed it looks likely that he is, but that lingering uncertainty justifies a deeper jury discussion.

At this point several jurors, including 8th, retire to the wash-room, temporarily dispelling the group tension. As 8th and 6th jurors converse there, 8th continues to restate the fact that it is his uncertainty about the case that is driving him, not any belief that the defendant is innocent: when 6th asks 'You think he's innocent?', 8th replies 'I don't know. It's possible' (p.22). This echoes the earlier discussion of the difference between possible and probable.

Key point

As they leave the wash-room, 6th Juror asks 8th to consider the implications of the jury delivering an incorrect 'not guilty' verdict and thus releasing a murderer back into the community. The stage direction here is important: '*8th Juror stands alone for a few moments and we know that this is the problem which has been tormenting him. He does not know, and never will*' (p.22). This is one of only a few stage directions describing characters' internal states, and it gives a key insight into 8th Juror's motivation, character and internal conflict. This highlights the play's concerns about human fallibility within the justice system.

In the continuing discussion, 8th Juror presents possible alternatives for who could have murdered the victim, given the victim's background. He also presents a series of reasons for the jury to doubt, or at least reconsider, the prosecution's evidence, asking them to question a number of details including:

- how the downstairs neighbour could be so sure it was the defendant's voice that he heard (p.24),
- whether the neighbour across the road could really have heard the defendant over the noise of the passing train (pp.25–6),

- whether the court-appointed defence lawyer had the motivation to provide a proper defence (p.29), and
- whether the defendant would have been so foolish as to shout 'I'm going to kill you' loudly enough for witnesses to hear, if he actually intended to kill the victim (p.28).

This last point initiates the climax of the play, which occurs at the end of the act (when 3rd Juror, in a moment of fury, threatens to kill 8th). 8th Juror argues that the phrase 'I'll kill you' is a common, empty threat that we all use regularly, and that it has become so meaningless that it shouldn't be used to convict the defendant in this case (p.28). 3rd Juror hotly disagrees, claiming that if someone yells the phrase angrily, as the defendant is said to have done, it is a clear indication that they truly mean to follow through on it (p.28). This argument will haunt him at the end of the act.

In the process of questioning the prosecution's case, and pointing out how much room there is for doubt, 8th Juror becomes aggressive for the first and only time in the play, becoming one of twelve 'angry men'. He is infuriated when 3rd and 12th jurors play tic-tac-toe rather than take the discussion (and their duty) seriously, and he violently snatches the page away from them. When this stimulates yet another argument with 3rd Juror and others, the Foreman steps in to try to maintain control and order (p.25).

Following this argument and a discussion regarding witness fallibility, 5th Juror voluntarily changes his opinion to 'not guilty', unprompted by a vote (p.28). After 3rd Juror's unfair accusations against him earlier in the scene, 5th Juror shows strength of character when he decides to publicly change his opinion: he is prepared to admit that he has reconsidered the case and has changed his mind, knowing this is likely to earn him denigration and criticism from fellow jurors. Although this does happen, primarily in 7th Juror's verbal attack (pp.28–9), 5th Juror's decision has another effect that is perhaps less expected: it seems to give others the courage to openly admit that the jury's preliminary conclusion was rushed and potentially incorrect. 11th Juror takes over 8th's role in the room for a moment, and for the first time someone other than 8th Juror asks the others to reconsider the 'facts' (p.29). On the strength of this new openness to discussion, 8th Juror calls for another vote and is rewarded when both 5th and 11th jurors change their votes to 'not guilty': the vote now stands at eight to four in favour of 'guilty' (p.31).

Q Why do characters in this unit exit to the washroom? How does this affect the scene?

Act One, Unit Five: Second exhibit (pp.31–3)

Summary: *11th Juror cites 'reasonable doubt' as his justification for changing his vote; 8th Juror requests to view another piece of evidence; the Guard brings in a diagram of the apartment.*

During this short section there is a distinct change in dynamics; 8th Juror is no longer driving the debate alone. For example, 5th Juror suddenly questions the testimony of the first witness, wanting to investigate the details of his statement. He wonders, specifically, whether the elderly gentleman was physically able to cover the distance necessary to reach the hallway in time to see the defendant, as his testimony claims.

No longer is the jury's task a clear one of trying to finalise a 'guilty' verdict. Instead, a significant 'reasonable doubt' has entered the debate – largely, although not entirely, instigated by 8th Juror.

The Guard delivers the map of the apartment requested by 8th Juror, and exits.

Key vocabulary

Dempsey-Firpo fight: a notorious 1923 New York boxing match, won by Jack Dempsey, although there was some controversy about a refereeing decision and the result has since been disputed. Luis Firpo was the first Latin-American boxer to challenge a heavyweight champion. As well as suggesting that 8th Juror is twisting accepted 'facts' in his argument, 7th Juror may be implying that 8th sympathises with social and cultural minority groups.

Act One, Unit Six: First demonstration (pp.33–7)

Summary: *8th Juror reconstructs a physical scenario to test the strength of a witness's testimony; the re-enactment suggests possible witness error; 3rd Juror's frustration peaks, climaxing in a verbal and attempted physical attack on 8th, who calmly uses the event to support his own argument.*

As the first act concludes, 8th Juror's interrogation of the evidence becomes less academic and speculative, as he sets up a reconstruction to measure the distances the elderly neighbour would have had to cover in order for his testimony to hold up. Predictably, given the increasing tension within the jury, this physical demonstration is met with open hostility from 10th, 7th, and 3rd jurors – the three most adamant supporters of the 'guilty' verdict. However, 8th Juror has the support of 11th, 5th, and 9th. Others remain uncertain, not yet committing themselves either to their original votes or to changing their minds. Some, like 6th Juror, seem willing to entertain the possibilities raised by the demonstration, volunteering the opinion that 8th Juror's proposal is 'possible' (p.36). Others (like 4th Juror and the Foreman) remain silent throughout the demonstration, neither objecting to nor supporting it.

The end of this unit, and of the first act, is a climax to both the conflict and the content of the play. During 8th Juror's experiment, 3rd's frustration and anger increase – he feels they are 'wasting time' (p.33) and 8th is being childish. Finally, at the end of the act, the conflict escalates to the point where 3rd Juror lunges in rage at 8th. When 5th and 6th jurors hold him back, 3rd angrily exclaims, 'Let go of me, God damn it! I'll kill him! I'll kill him!' (p.37). Far from feeling threatened, 8th Juror calmly uses the incident to enforce his earlier point (from p.28) that such a threat made in anger should not necessarily incriminate an individual. This contrasts with 3rd Juror's own earlier assertion that such a threat was incontrovertible evidence against the defendant, because if anyone 'says a thing like that ... they mean it' (p.28).

This moment of physical aggression brings the conflict in the play from an emotional level to a more concrete level, and leaves the audience at a heightened level of involvement just before the interval.

Q Imagine you are in the audience at a production of the play. What kinds of conversations might you have in the foyer at interval – how would you predict the play might end? Which characters are you drawn to, and why?

Q If you were in the jury, what would your vote be at this point?

Act Two, Unit Seven: Fourth vote (pp.38–40)

Summary: *Evening arrives and the storm approaches; another vote is called; the vote now stands at six votes each way.*

This unit returns us to the play after the interval (it would be unusual for a production not to put an interval between the two acts). Although the audience has had a break, no time has passed in the chronology of the play, and the second act continues exactly where the first left off. There is a sense of discomfort and embarrassment following the outburst and emotional climax of Act One. The jurors make small talk to hide their discomfort, until 6th Juror calls for another vote. The count this time is taken openly, with each juror calling out his vote, suggesting that in the heightened conflict, there is somehow an increased trust and lack of artifice amongst the jury – there is no need to vote secretly anymore, as they have all become more openly vulnerable with each other.

The vote reveals that 2nd and 6th jurors have both changed their minds, so that the verdict is now split equally with six votes each way. This evenness gives an illusion of stability and calmness, especially after the emotional volatility of the previous scene, but really it represents a tension and a tipping point. The perfect balance between the two sides of the vote indicates that there is strength on both sides, and that while the 'not guilty' vote is slowly gaining support, the debate is far from over. This is paralleled in the physical environment outside the room: as 5th Juror notes, 'We're gonna have a storm' (p.39). Clearly this refers not just to the weather, but to the emotional exchange that remains in the play.

Act Two, Unit Eight: Second demonstration (pp.40–7)

Summary: *The storm breaks; 3rd Juror defends his earlier outburst; the jury's arguments begin to get personal; 8th Juror conducts another demonstration (this time with 4th's help) to support his argument for 'reasonable doubt'.*

As the tension in the room has increased steadily throughout the play, so has the heat and the climactic atmosphere outside, until it becomes '*oppressively still*' (p.40), just before the storm finally breaks (p.41). The Foreman wonders if the rain will 'cool things off' (p.41), speaking literally about the weather with an earnestness and enthusiasm that allows little room for metaphor. The audience, though, wonder whether the rain will have symbolic properties and 'cool off' the tension and tempers too. And for a few moments it does seem to. The Foreman indulges in an irrelevant reminiscence about a baseball game, and the jurors find that they are able to turn the fan on and gain some relief from the literal heat.

But the moment of calm is temporary, and the discussion in the washroom, where several jurors have gathered, returns to the case and how to finalise the verdict. While several jurors, including 10th and 7th, are in favour of declaring a hung jury rather than being forced to continue with the process, this preference does not prevail and 8th Juror soon raises another point for debate. This time, he questions the strength of the evidence of the defendant's inability to remember details of the film he claims he saw after leaving his apartment. As he did with 3rd Juror's outburst, 8th Juror finds that he is able to support his argument by relying on the resources available: the other jurors. He conducts a simple experiment showing that 4th Juror is unable to accurately recall details of a movie he recently saw. Evidence for 'reasonable doubt' about the prosecution's case is mounting strongly, and the jurors finally agree to spend one more hour in the debate.

Q Why does Rose include the Foreman's long speech about the baseball game (p.41), and what can we learn about the play and its individual characters from this apparently unrelated anecdote?

Q The storm is one of few symbolic strategies Rose uses to enhance themes and action in this play. Why is the approaching storm important and how does it help us understand what is going on in the play at this point?

Act Two, Unit Nine: Third demonstration (pp.47–50)

Summary: *2nd Juror questions the prosecution's argument about the direction of the stab wound; 3rd demonstrates the stabbing motion using 8th Juror (stopping just short of stabbing him); 5th Juror contradicts this with his knowledge of switch-knives; 7th Juror decides to vote 'not guilty'; 8th Juror calls for another vote.*

As the play's conclusion nears, the balance has shifted so that 3rd and 10th jurors are now defending themselves against a majority. They stand firm in their beliefs and their 'guilty' votes, despite mounting justification for reasonable doubt, to which 2nd Juror contributes by questioning the evidence of the stab wound. For a moment 3rd Juror is able to regain power, both figuratively (demonstrating how a wound *could* be made by a short man against a taller man) and literally (wielding the dangerous weapon against 8th Juror). But this is short-lived, as 5th Juror quickly steps in. Drawing on his own personal experience and upbringing in a rough area, he shows how the knife would actually be wielded in the opposite direction. This information discredits 3rd Juror's argument (p.49).

Key point

The visual image of 3rd Juror almost stabbing 8th (p.48) is a powerful moment of drama in this play, presenting a concise portrait of the relationship between the two men. It symbolises 3rd Juror's constant attempts to discredit 8th's arguments. It also encapsulates 8th's attitude to conflict and his relationship with his antagonist: he calmly stands his ground and, in doing so, appears the stronger of the two. Had he attempted to fight back or even resist, perhaps one of them might have been injured with the knife.

Around this point, 7th Juror decides to change his vote. He initially claims that it is because he has 'had enough' (p.50) and wants to get out, but he is quickly forced to admit that in fact he now agrees with 8th Juror that there is cause for reasonable doubt about the defendant's guilt. In fact, not only does he doubt the defendant's guilt, but 7th Juror actually appears to believe in his innocence, saying 'I – don't think he's guilty' (p.50). Straight away another vote is called for.

Q Now that 3rd and 10th are in a minority and not a safe majority, what changes are evident in their speech and behaviour?

Act Two, Unit Ten: Fifth vote (pp.51–4)

Summary: *The jury votes by show of hands; 12th Juror and the Foreman change their votes so the vote stands at nine to three in favour of 'not guilty'; 10th Juror resorts to class stereotypes and aggression in an attempt to frighten others and win the argument; another vote is called for.*

This short unit shows 10th Juror's desperate bid to win back some of the jury who have defected to the 'not guilty' camp. His long speeches denouncing those of the lower socio-economic classes (pp.51–2 and pp.52–3) reflect his earlier opinions but now seem fuelled by his own fear and anger, and motivated by an attempt to frighten the rest of the jury. These motivations contrast with the calm, rational approach that 8th Juror has taken all along. In his desperation, 10th Juror's argument is an emotional appeal to others' fears; his justification for convicting the defendant has become 'if we don't smack them down whenever we can, then they are gonna own us', and we need to 'get him before his kind gets us' (p.53).

During these final moments of the jury's deliberations, and of the play, 10th Juror makes no attempt to conceal his prejudices or the fact that he doesn't particularly care whether or not the defendant committed this particular crime. He simply wants him convicted as a representative of an entire social group, so the punishment may serve as an example to that group.

8th Juror summarises the purpose and effect of the 'reasonable doubt' clause of the judge's instructions to the jury, reminding us that even while he and the other jurors now 'seem to feel that the defendant is innocent', they do not have to be certain (p.53). They need only believe, on the basis of the evidence and the arguments presented by the prosecution, that he *could* reasonably be innocent.

It is 3rd Juror who calls for the final vote.

Q In this unit the extent of 10th Juror's prejudices are revealed. How does Rose relate prejudice to fear?

Act Two, Unit Eleven: Sixth vote (pp.54–8, ends when 10th Juror says '"Not guilty." Do whatever you want.')

Summary: *12th Juror changes his mind back to 'guilty'; they agree to discuss a hung jury if they can't resolve the vote by 7pm; 9th Juror deduces that the second witness needs glasses and thus her testimony is questionable; 12th Juror changes his vote again; 10th Juror changes his vote to 'not guilty'.*

The vote called for at the conclusion of the previous unit never takes place as the arguments overtake the formal side of proceedings. Yet during this unit the individual votes are discussed several times. First, 12th Juror revokes his 'not guilty' vote and, as the possibility of a hung jury is discussed, 9th Juror sees 4th rubbing his nose (where his glasses pinch him) and remembers the second witness doing the same, although she was not wearing glasses in court. The assertion that she wears glasses calls into question the validity of her testimony and, as with each previous investigation of 'facts' from the court case, this has the effect of changing a juror's mind. At this point 12th Juror changes his opinion back again to 'not guilty'. (The discussion of the second witness also contributes to 4th Juror's change of mind in the next unit.) At this point, 10th Juror also changes his mind – not because he is convinced by the arguments, but because he is simply worn down, it seems, and unwilling to continue fighting any longer for his belief in the face of such an overwhelming majority.

Key vocabulary

J. Walter Thompson: an American advertising pioneer around the turn of the twentieth century.

Clarence Darrow: an American defence lawyer best known for some of his successful 1920s cases, including one in which he defended two teenage boys who pleaded guilty to a murder charge. The case is renowned for Darrow's long, emotive, persuasive and poetic summation, after which the judge sentenced the boys to life imprisonment instead of the electric chair.

Q 12th Juror is the only one to change his vote more than once. What does this tell us about his character, and how is he different to the others?

Act Two, Unit Twelve: Verdict (pp.58–9)

Summary: *4th Juror changes his vote; 3rd makes a last stand then changes his vote; the Foreman informs the Guard and they exit to deliver their verdict; the rain has ceased.*

In the final pages of the play, 4th Juror changes his vote, having been swayed towards reasonable doubt by the argument about the second witness and her eyesight. 3rd Juror now stands alone, just as 8th did at the start of the play, voting against the other eleven jurors. He delivers a long speech reiterating his reasons for his convictions, and as with previous reasonings, these rely on information about character, evidence, and personal intuition. None of the other jurors is willing to speak until 8th Juror intimates that 3rd's opinions are being influenced and even confused by his own relationship with his son. After a long pause, 3rd Juror finally changes his vote so that the jury have at last achieved a unanimous opinion. They inform the guard that they are ready to deliver a verdict to the court.

Two important moments remain for the swift denouement of the play. The first is a silent exchange between 3rd and 8th Jurors – the last two left in the room. 8th Juror brings 3rd his jacket and helps him put it on (p.59). This motion balances the earlier incidents when 3rd Juror tried to attack (p.37) and almost stabbed 8th (p.48): the early incidents are moments of conflict, and this one is a moment of resolution and closure. It is typical that 8th Juror is the one to extend a gesture of assistance, compassion and gentleness, and it is also symbolic that 3rd – having finally relinquished his long-held opposition to the 'not guilty' vote – no longer has any desire or capacity to resist. He accepts the gesture (though does not return it in any way) and departs, leaving 8th Juror to a final survey of the room. He leaves his knife stuck in the table, leaving his mark on the case, leaving his argument behind him, letting go of the evening's proceedings.

Finally, the rain ends: a sign that the conflict and tension have ceased, and that the situation has been resolved.

Q Why do you think 3rd Juror finally changes his vote?

CHARACTERS & RELATIONSHIPS

8th Juror

Key quotes

'It's not easy for me to raise my hand and send a boy off to die without talking about it first.' (p.7)

'*9th Juror half rises but then feels 8th Juror's hand firmly on his arm, gently pulling him down.*' (Stage direction, p.8)

'I kept putting myself in the boy's place.' (p.14)

'*... this is the problem which has been tormenting him. He does not know, and never will.*' (Stage direction, p.22)

'I'm telling you, if this guy was sitting ringside at the Dempsey-Firpo fight, he'd be tryin' to tell us Firpo won.' (7th Juror about 8th, p.32)

8th Juror, an architect and father of two, is the only juror to vote 'not guilty' in the first instance. Amongst these twelve anonymous men, he is the first to really gain the audience's attention, willingly and publicly going against the majority of the group by voting 'not guilty' after all the others vote 'guilty' (p.7). In this early action, we can identify many important qualities of his character. He is willing to question the 'facts' with which he has been presented. He has compassion for the accused. He is taking his duty seriously, and is prepared to spend time discussing the case rather than deferring to an overwhelming majority opinion. He has a confidence that allows him to express his opinions and beliefs even in the face of unanimous disagreement from his peers.

His confidence is a quiet one, however, and he never uses aggression, violence or any form of intimidation to push his arguments. Instead, as he suggests immediately after the vote, logic and communication are his tools: 'Well, I guess we talk' (p.7). He is not interested in steamrolling others to change their minds, but he has a reasonable doubt about the defendant's guilt, and wants to be sure that the jurors have given due consideration to the case before condemning a young man to death. As he says, 'It's just that we're talking about somebody's life here. I mean, we can't decide in five minutes. Suppose we're wrong?' (p.7).

8th Juror is the only character who does not change his vote throughout the jury's deliberations. Each of the others is eventually compelled to change his mind at least once (12th Juror changes his three times), usually thanks to an argument posited by 8th. Yet while he is firm in his position, he is not inflexible. Rather, he regularly and openly admits his own uncertainties, frequently answering others' questions with an honest 'I don't know'; by not hiding his vulnerability he ultimately wins over the entire jury. Similarly, when he first justifies his vote of 'not guilty', he states 'I haven't got anything brilliant. I only know as much as you do' (p.13). Rather than trying to position himself as an authority on the case or the facts, or build himself up by criticising or belittling others, 8th Juror's strength lies in the way that he gradually convinces the jurors that *none* of them can be certain of the facts, and so the jury must admit reasonable doubt regarding the defendant's guilt and therefore return a verdict of 'not guilty'.

Charisma

It is easy for an audience to empathise with 8th Juror. He endorses many personal qualities that are traditionally seen as desirable character traits. These include:

- compassion – he is committed to ensuring a fair trial for the defendant (who is from a less privileged background); he is also compassionate towards his fellow jurors,
- courtesy – he is one of few characters who address others as 'Mr' or 'gentleman',

- reasonableness – he is always careful to consider any possibilities offered up in discussion, and to take time to investigate each idea,
- integrity and commitment – he never shifts from his 'not guilty' vote (although he is open to having his mind changed if the evidence is strong enough), and
- open-mindedness – although he admits that, on the face of it, the defendant looks guilty, he refuses to act on assumptions or prejudices.

These traits not only make him a sympathetic character for the audience, but ultimately enable him to convince each and every jury member to change his vote to 'not guilty'. He does not do this alone, however, because as the jury members gradually change their minds, others begin to question the evidence in the same way, gathering support for the 'not guilty' vote.

Key point

Although 8th Juror is clearly presented as a likeable, charismatic and strong character, he is never simplified and portrayed as perfect, but rather as human and therefore fallible. An example is when he admits to breaking the law and purchasing the switch-knife in order to show that the knife in evidence was not as unique as the prosecution claimed it to be (p.16–17). He freely admits to breaking the law, and we are left to decide for ourselves whether his intentions here mitigate his crime.

Not only are 8th Juror's actions and speeches consistent throughout the play, but in the very first and last moments we are given indications in the stage directions as to the essence of his character. The first direction for 8th Juror, preceding his very first line, is *'smiling'*. No other character has such a warm introduction. At the other end of the play, he is the last to leave the stage, and his final action is one of kindness as he helps 3rd Juror put on his jacket (p.59). This simple act reminds us that 8th Juror is a character who, however flawed, is always compassionate and considerate towards his fellow human beings.

Physicality

Physically, 8th Juror is presented as a gentle, calm and quiet character. In stage directions his movements are careful, purposeful, reasoned and considered. His only moment of physical aggression is when he notices 12th and 3rd jurors playing tic-tac-toe and he 'snatches' the page and throws it away (p.25).

8th Juror's speech is another aspect of his physicality. Although the stage directions regarding delivery of lines in this play are few, there are other ways in which Rose is able to convey to actors and directors how the line should be spoken. Examples include the following.

Pauses: The stage direction *'pause'* before or within a speech suggests that a character is feeling thoughtful or has some hesitance or uncertainty about what they are saying, but at the same time indicates that they have the confidence to pause and consider the point rather than just rushing ahead and saying something in order to fill the silence. 8th Juror pauses before or during several speeches, while other characters rarely do.

Punctuation: Lines ending in exclamation marks are clearly intended to be delivered with more urgency, force and perhaps volume than those ending in full stops. 8th Juror's lines rarely end in exclamation marks, even on the one occasion when he appears to lose his temper for a moment (p.25). This is a notable contrast with other characters, whose lines regularly contain several exclamation marks.

Interruptions: If the script directs a character to interrupt another character's line, this is an indication that the interruption is usually urgent, loud and agitated in some way. It also indicates a lack of respect for the first speaker, and usually takes place in moments of heightened conflict. Although 8th Juror is interrupted several times by other characters, he never interrupts others while they are speaking.

Q What other physical behaviours or speech patterns help develop and reveal 8th Juror's character?

3rd Juror

Key quotes

'... let's get this over with. We've probably all got things to do.' (p.3)

'You bet I'm excitable. We're trying to put a guilty man in the chair where he belongs and all of a sudden somebody's telling us fairy tales – and we're listening.' (p.20)

Key quotes

'You're a sadist!' (8th Juror to 3rd Juror, p.37)

'I don't care whether I'm alone or not. It's my right ... You're not goin' to intimidate me. I'm entitled to my opinion. I can sit in this goddam room for a year.' (p.58)

3rd Juror is the final juror to change his vote, holding strongly to his beliefs throughout. He aggressively, impatiently and often sarcastically rejects the alternative explanations and possibilities raised by 8th and other jurors.

It is notable that 3rd Juror is resistant for so long to the arguments proposed by 8th and, increasingly, the other jurors. It creates an interesting internal tension within his character: from the opening moments of the play he is impatient to get the decision over with and to leave the room, yet he is the juror who holds out for the longest, drawing the proceedings out. This indicates that he is quite committed to his opinion that the defendant is guilty, otherwise he would simply have changed his vote swiftly so as to get out of the room.

Aggression and violence

3rd Juror is assertive, confident, competitive and both verbally and physically aggressive. He is described by 6th Juror as a 'loud, heavy-set guy' (p.22). In the first few pages we learn a little about his background – he is the proud manager of a business that he has built up himself, having 'started with nothing' (p.4), and this is not his first experience of jury duty (p.3). He doesn't speak a great deal during the early part of the play, but when he does it tends to consist of irritable and impatient comments gradually leaning towards anger, such as in his outburst about his own son (p.12).

This outburst reveals a lot about his relationship with his son, and helps us to understand some of the influences on his interpretation of the 'facts' in the case at hand. He feels that his son is representative of a contemporary generation who lack respect for their elders; it seems likely at this stage that this is the way he views the defendant too. At the very end of the play, 8th Juror articulates this conflation between 3rd Juror's son and the defendant when he says, 'It's not your boy. He's somebody else.' 3rd Juror does not argue (p.59).

The outburst on page 12 also helps us understand several central facets of 3rd Juror's character. In his description of the incident with his sixteen-year-old son four years earlier, he reveals that a common way of handling conflict in his family has always been with physical violence. He and his son 'had a battle' and the son hit him in the face (p.12). This was obviously not a one-off incident, and nor was the violence confined to the son's behaviour. There is evidence of domestic violence from 3rd Juror, such as when he told his then nine-year-old son: 'I'm gonna make a man outa you or I'm gonna bust you in half trying' (p.12). This threat indicates his dependence on violence as a problem-solving strategy. This story about his son also informs us about 3rd Juror's priorities: the reason he was so angry is that his son ran away from a fight. This attitude shows that he thinks violence and aggression are markers of masculinity, and that any avoidance of such things is cowardly and shameful. It is easy to see, then, that 3rd Juror will have little respect for 8th's non-combative and academic approach to resolving the conflict within the jury-room.

Stubbornness or integrity?

Every step of the way, 3rd Juror resists 8th's attempts to question the prosecution's argument by reviewing all the 'facts' of the case. Instead he holds firm to his original belief in the defendant's guilt. As far as he is concerned, the case is 'one of those open and shut things' (p.7); he can see no value in revisiting the evidence and the witness testimonies, as 8th Juror proceeds to do.

3rd Juror has an unshakeable faith in the legal system and the case's lawyers, and can't imagine why anyone would question the arguments presented in court. He is reluctant to admit the possibility that witnesses might have made mistakes, or that the defendant's court-appointed lawyer might not have done the most thorough job possible. Instead, he persists in taking at face value, and clinging to, the evidence presented by the prosecution. He has made up his mind, early on, to be convinced by the prosecution's case. Even by the end of the play he is still relying on their arguments for the defendant's guilt ('every single thing that came out in that courtroom ... says he's guilty', p.58), refusing to concede to any of the alternatives 8th and other jurors have presented during the course of the deliberation.

His stubbornness tends to turn audiences against him, because we find 8th Juror's attitude of flexibility and humility more appealing. But viewed from a slightly different perspective, 3rd Juror could be considered one of the most consistent and admirable characters in the play. He holds firm to his own beliefs, even when he has to stand alone against the others, despite being desperately keen for the situation to be resolved.

Crisis points

3rd Juror faces two major crisis points during the course of the play. Both are important moments not just for him, but for the outcome of the deliberation.

Key point

Both of 3rd Juror's crisis points occur at the end of an act, and as such he is the character most responsible for shaping the action of the play. The first crisis point, at the end of the first act, raises the stakes and leaves the audience in a heightened state for the interval. The second is *Twelve Angry Men*'s final moment of crisis, which is followed by an extremely swift denouement and the conclusion of the play.

The first crisis point is the conflict at the end of the first act, when 3rd Juror's frustration with 8th's arguments peaks and he explodes with 'Let go of me, God damn it! I'll kill him! I'll kill him!' (p.37). Earlier, noting that the defendant allegedly yelled 'I'm going to kill you' at his father, 8th Juror argues that people say things like that 'every day. It doesn't mean we're going to kill someone' (p.28). But 3rd Juror passionately declares that 'Anybody says a thing like that ... they mean it' (p.28). This line foreshadows the impact of the moment when he says just such a thing to 8th Juror.

Not only is this physically and emotionally the most dramatic moment in the script so far, it serves several other important purposes. These include:

- revealing 3rd Juror's extreme and violent tendencies (yet simultaneously earning our sympathy, as he undermines himself in his own passion),
- increasing our empathy and respect for 8th Juror, who stands calm and firm against 3rd's hysteria, not using the moment to make him feel any worse but instead allowing 3rd's behaviour to speak for itself, and

- neatly demonstrating for the audience the weakness of one of the primary aspects of the prosecution's evidence.

This is a powerful moment, providing a strong physical demonstration for the audience, in contrast to the many other moments of verbal argument. It is also a demonstration that – unlike the staged re-enactments such as 8th Juror's attempt to time the elderly witness's walk – arises organically out of the interactions between characters, thus having the potential to take the audience by surprise and generate an even stronger reaction.

The second crisis point for 3rd Juror is not just a moment of personal crisis, but also has implications for the progression of the narrative. It occurs at the end of the play (pp.58–9) and includes his final long speech and eventual decision to change his vote. During this last speech, claiming that he can 'sit in this goddam room for a year' and never change his mind (p.58), there are three separate stage directions noting that the rest of the jurors remain silent. The poignancy of this moment is clear: 3rd Juror is making a last attempt to maintain his status and to convict the defendant. But the rest of the room is against him now, and he has been weakened by the process; when he gives in he does so extremely quickly and unequivocally. All his protests throughout the play boil down to the single line where he changes his mind, 'All right. "Not guilty".' (p. 59). The denouement after this final resolution of conflict takes only seconds: nothing is left for the jury to do but leave the room to deliver their verdict.

Q How does Rose ensure that we judge 3rd Juror's stubbornness as a negative instead of a positive character trait?

Central binary: 3rd and 8th jurors

Key quotes

3rd Juror: (*leaning over towards 8th Juror*) Well, look, do you really think he's innocent?

8th Juror: I don't know. (p.7)

8th Juror: I'm not asking anyone to accept it. I'm just saying that it's possible.

3rd Juror: (*shouting*) And I'm saying it's not possible. (p.16)

Equal and opposite

3rd and 8th jurors each provide a foil for the other. They are almost equally matched in determination: each holds onto his original vote until the final moments of the play when 3rd changes his mind. Both are passionate about their points of view, and more vocal and active than most other characters – who sometimes seem to just go along for the ride, changing their votes once convinced by some argument or other. Throughout the play, 3rd and 8th jurors each represent one extreme on the continuum of opinions about the defendant's guilt. In between, all the other jurors agree with one or other of them at some point, with 12th Juror vacillating the most, changing his vote three separate times.

Relationship

The conflict between 3rd and 8th jurors is based not just on their differing opinions of the defendant's guilt, but also on their different interpersonal styles. 3rd Juror is constantly frustrated by 8th's slow and patient approach, his willingness to re-examine evidence and his regular admissions that he does not honestly know whether or not the defendant is guilty of this crime. For his part, 8th only becomes angry on one occasion: when he catches 12th and 3rd jurors playing tic-tac-toe. It is significant that the only incident that provokes 8th to aggression is 3rd Juror's inattention and apparent lack of respect for the task at hand. The conflict between the two represents the broader conflict throughout the play.

The two are as different as possible when it comes to interpersonal interactions. As discussed previously, 8th Juror is calm, reasoned, analytical and courteous. In contrast, 3rd Juror tends towards aggression, rudeness, violence, impatience and narrow-mindedness. The exchange that best highlights the differences in character occurs when 8th Juror volunteers to be the pretend 'victim' in 3rd's re-enactment of the fatal stabbing motion. According to stage directions, *'8th Juror and 3rd Juror look steadily at each other, then 3rd Juror suddenly stabs downward, hard'* (p.48). This moment perfectly characterises the relationship between the two: 3rd Juror is physically aggressive and is regularly 'on the attack' in terms of his responses to others' questions and suggestions. On the other hand, 8th Juror nearly always remains calm, never backing away from his commitment to reasonable doubt, even in the face of 'attack' from others. As well as symbolically illustrating the nature of their conflict, it foreshadows how that conflict will ultimately be resolved: since 8th Juror will not relinquish his position, 3rd is ultimately forced to step down, changing his vote.

Key point

It is significant that 3rd Juror does not actually follow through with his action and wound 8th: this was never his intention. Instead, he had hoped to intimidate him and prove his own point in the process. Again, this illustrates 3rd Juror's attitude to 8th and to the case in general: it is not his desire to hurt others, rather to overpower them and convince them that he is right.

Q The relationship between 3rd and 8th jurors is the central one in the play. Identify other important relationships between characters and discuss how they differ from this one.

THEMES, IDEAS & VALUES

Fallibility and memory

Key quotes

'They're only people. People make mistakes. Could they be wrong?' (p.14)

'He wouldn't really lie. But perhaps he'd make himself believe that he'd heard those words and recognised the boy's face.' (p.27)

'Witnesses can make mistakes.' (p.31)

'He's an old man ... Half the time he was confused. How could he be positive about anything?' (p.33)

'Maybe she honestly thought she saw the boy kill his father. I say that she saw only a blur.' (p.57)

In a case where most of the evidence is comprised of eyewitness testimony, a key factor in the jury's decision will be the perceived reliability of the witnesses. In *Twelve Angry Men*, discussions about the verdict and therefore about the evidence often revolve around the eyewitness testimony. The jurors rarely accuse witnesses of any intentional inaccuracy, but they do regularly discuss the likelihood of witnesses being fallible – capable of making mistakes.

Research into eyewitness accuracy

The reliability of eyewitness testimony is a concern that underpins many legal situations. Most people hold an intuitive and informal belief that eyewitness testimony is one of the most reliable forms of evidence. We tend to place great faith in what we have witnessed ourselves – just think of common phrases like 'I saw it with my own eyes' and 'before your very eyes'. This emphasises the power that witness testimony can have over jury members: as 4th Juror says about the second witness, 'As far as I can see, this is unshakeable testimony' and 3rd Juror agrees: 'That's the whole case' (p.54). Contemporary western culture gives considerable weight to empirical evidence and physical events we can experience with the senses. However, the reliability of eyewitness testimony has been questioned and challenged all over the world, and studies have repeatedly demonstrated that eyewitness testimonies of events are very commonly inaccurate. 9th Juror makes a strong argument for the second witness's eyesight being impaired, thus undermining the strength of her testimony and, by extension, the prosecution's case.

One of the best-known researchers into human memory and its role in eyewitness testimony is psychologist Elizabeth Loftus, author of *Eyewitness Testimony* (1979). This book examines the processes and consequences of human recall and memory in legal situations. In it she notes that 'Jurors have been known to accept eyewitness testimony pointing to guilt even when it is *far* outweighed by evidence of innocence' (p.9), and cites her own studies replicating this finding. While the book was published after Rose's original television script, Loftus was not the first to explore the possibilities of witness fallibility, so Rose's focus on the witnesses' reliability in *Twelve Angry Men* would not have been startling to audiences at the time.

Inaccuracies of eyewitness testimony may be attributable to many factors, including

- trauma and stress influencing perception of events, and therefore interfering with the formation or recall of accurate memory;
- general and genuine human error in recall;
- the disruptive and sometimes reconstructive effects of exposure to facts after the event;
- intentional or unintentional leading questions to witnesses;
- intentional fabrication by witnesses.

Many of these possible causes of witness error are explored in *Twelve Angry Men*. 9th Juror suggests it is possible that in order to 'be recognised, to be listened to, to be quoted just once' (p.27), the first witness subconsciously convinced himself he really had heard the defendant shouting before the murder.

But the play is not an exploration of how or why eyewitnesses might provide false evidence. What is important is not how these errors come about, but the fact that witness testimony is demonstrably fallible.

To err is human ...

8th Juror repeatedly questions the reliability of the case witnesses. He does so with no malevolence or judgement: he merely wants other jurors to consider the fact that people do make mistakes, and to remember that in this case, such mistakes could cost a young boy his life. As he points out, the witnesses are 'the entire case for the prosecution' (p.14), so he wants to make sure that the jury is confident, beyond reasonable doubt, that the witness testimonies were absolutely accurate. The fact that the absolute accuracy of such testimonies is difficult, if not impossible, to establish, forms the basis for 8th Juror's argument for reasonable doubt.

The jurors who object to the possibilities of witness error seem to take the suggestion personally, and defend the witnesses' reputations as though they were defending their own. For example, when discussing the first witness's reliability, 10th Juror objects: 'You're makin' out like it don't matter what people say' (p.31). He appears afraid that if the possibility of human error is admitted, then he might never be able to trust anyone again, or, perhaps more importantly, *he* might never be trusted again.

Demonstration

The possibility of witness error or fallible human memory is not just used to discredit the certainty of witness evidence, but also to strengthen the defendant's case. In court, the boy could not recall details of the film he claims to have been watching at the time of the murder, which leads the jurors to doubt his alibi. 4th Juror argues that the only possible reason for this memory lapse is that 'he wasn't there that night' (p.44). He rejects 8th Juror's suggestion that perhaps the 'great emotional stress' of his father's death compromised the boy's memory (p.45). However, 8th Juror proceeds to demonstrate that even in mundane situations, human error is possible: 4th finds himself unable to remember the details of a film he had recently seen. While 4th Juror is not swayed by this demonstration, still convinced of the defendant's guilt, the episode offers the audience a compelling illustration of genuine human fallibility. This leads us to judge those characters in the play who refuse to accept the possibility of witness error.

Implications

Twelve Angry Men never suggests that human fallibility in itself is a negative trait. Instead, by presenting it through the perspective of the rational, reasonable 8th Juror, Rose argues that human fallibility is a fact we must accept. Fallibility should always be taken into account when we are making judgements on a situation, especially when these judgements occur in the legal context with the power to determine life or death. Rose allows 8th Juror to demonstrate for us the realities of error and inaccuracies of memory, and in doing so undermines those characters who remain completely convinced by eyewitness testimony. Thus the play provides a gentle critique of a judicial system that allows convictions based solely on witness evidence.

Q Can you think of an incident from your own life where your memory of the event has been shown to be inaccurate? Has this changed your certainty about your own memories on other occasions?

The value of facts

Key quotes

'You can't refute facts.' (p.10)

'Facts may be coloured by the personalities of the people who present them.' (p.27)

'Sometimes the facts that are staring you in the face are wrong!' (p.29)

'I'm sick and tired of facts. You can twist 'em any way you like. Know what I mean?' (p.40)

A 'fact' is defined as an event that has actually occurred, a 'truth known by actual experience or observation' (Macquarie Dictionary). Like witness testimonies, 'facts' in a court case (as in more general situations) are often seen as irrefutable evidence, carrying great weight in any argument. Facts can be powerful and convincing but, as this play illustrates, they are not always what they appear to be. Not only are the 'facts' of the case in *Twelve Angry Men* gradually disputed in the course of the play, but they have been largely extracted from witness testimony, which, as we have seen, are subject to human error or misinterpretation.

While many of the jurors are convinced by, and persistently rely on, the 'facts' of this case, 8th Juror slowly works his way through the facts as they know them, demonstrating that because many cannot actually be proven, they cannot be used to convict the defendant.

Understandably, not all the jurors are happy to have their 'facts' discredited in front of them. Without those facts to cling to, it quickly becomes apparent that not one juror can truly be certain about what happened and whether or not the defendant committed the crime. While 8th Juror is relatively comfortable admitting uncertainty, other jurors' reactions indicate that they feel threatened by it, leading them to resist for as long as possible.

When is a fact not a fact?

The word 'fact' is loosely tossed about the jury-room without much thought for its meaning by most of the jurors, apart from 8th. Very frequently, statements like 'we heard the facts, didn't we?' (p.8), 'there are facts staring you right in your face' (p.28) or 'pay attention to the facts' (p.31) are uttered, but are not followed up with any detail about what those facts are. When facts *are* detailed, they appear convincing at first. Some 'facts' the prosecution presented, cited by 4th Juror as evidence for the defendant's guilt, include:

- the fact that the murder weapon was the boy's knife – a knife so unique that 'the storekeeper who sold it to him identified the knife in court and said it was the only one of its kind he had ever had in stock' (p.15) and
- the fact that friends of the defendant identified the weapon as the same knife the defendant owned (p.15).

While these two facts convince the jurors, and are likely to convince an audience too, 8th Juror is able to discredit both when he demonstrates the ease with which he was able to acquire an identical knife (p.16).

Demonstration

As with his illustration concerning human memory, 8th Juror provides a concrete example of how a 'fact' might turn out not to be 'true' after all. Regarding the murder weapon, he argues that 'it's possible that the boy lost the knife and that someone else stabbed his father with a similar knife' (p.16). None of the jurors accept this possibility, and at this point the audience is inclined to agree with them, as Rose deliberately makes his proposal sound very unlikely. However, 8th Juror reveals an identical knife moments later. Both the jury and the audience are now forced to concede that the 'fact' of the unusual knife being unique, and thus incriminating, is no longer a 'fact' at all.

Key point

Note that before revealing the knife, 8th Juror says of his proposal: 'I'm not asking anyone to accept it. I'm just saying that it's possible' (p.16). This reminds us that his endeavour is never to prove the defendant's innocence, but to demonstrate *reasonable doubt* about his guilt.

Devaluation of the word

The term 'fact' is gradually stripped of its power during the course of the play, so that by the time it is used by 10th Juror to describe stereotyped characteristics of particular socio-economic groups, Rose convinces us to recognise 'fact' as a completely subjective construct. 10th Juror uses the word in all earnestness, saying

> let's talk facts. These people are born to lie ... They don't know what the truth is ... They think different. They act different. Well, for instance, they don't need any big excuse to kill someone ... Well, that's true. Everybody knows it. (p.51)

Clearly, these are not 'facts' but prejudiced opinions. By association, then, all other notions identified as 'facts' in this case can now also be viewed as biased opinions and reports.

Implications

As with witness testimony, the effect of the focus on 'fact' in *Twelve Angry Men* is to endorse the view that we should consider all available evidence when faced with important decisions. The implication is that we should never take things at face value, even when they appear to be facts. As 8th Juror demonstrates, new evidence can destroy a fact, just as personal bias can colour the truth of an event, whether by intent or accident. Rose's play demonstrates that unquestioning belief is a dangerous habit (in this case, it would have sent a young boy to his death without anyone ever questioning whether he was truly guilty of the crime). He challenges audiences to question their assumptions, opinions and faith, not just about the specific details of this case but, by extension, about our own lives.

Q Does Rose suggest that there can be no such thing as a 'fact', or does he simply argue that it is difficult to establish the truth of any given 'fact'?

Prejudice and stereotypes

Key quotes

'Children from slum backgrounds are potential menaces to society.' (p.12)

'He's a common, ignorant slob. He don't even speak good English.' (p.28)

'I don't think the kind of boy he is has anything to do with it. The facts are supposed to determine the case.' (p.40)

'These people are born to lie ... They are different ... they're very big drinkers ... nobody's blaming them for it. That's how they are, by nature, y'know what I mean?' (p.51–2)

'It's very hard to keep personal prejudice out of a thing like this. And no matter where you run into it, prejudice obscures the truth.' (p.53)

While the play is not explicitly political in its examination of characters, attitudes and conflicts, it does value human compassion over narrow-mindedness and bigotry. It does this by endowing 8th Juror – the most sympathetic and likeable character – with qualities of empathy, tolerance and sensitivity, while leaving the prejudicial attitudes to the more aggressive, argumentative and difficult characters – particularly 10th Juror.

The compassion displayed by 8th Juror from the very first vote, when he refuses to convict the defendant without a reasonable discussion even though the boy certainly appears guilty, sets a moral tone for the play. *Twelve Angry Men* is never didactic, but by repeatedly associating prejudice with the less sympathetic characters, it encourages us to judge and condemn such behaviour.

Class stereotypes

We know that the defendant and the victim are from a disadvantaged socio-economic background – early in the jurors' discussions, they review details of the case including the defendant's background. The jurors describe a slum upbringing and a tough environment. Characters repeatedly attribute the defendant's violent behaviour to his upbringing. While there may be some validity in this cause-and-effect theory, there are no statistics, studies or 'facts' to support the causation, so the opinions here are only ever *stereotypes*: inflexible and generalised assumptions about a particular group.

Other stereotypes

There are examples of prejudice based on other characteristics too, including:

- race – 7th Juror attacks 11th: '... he comes over to this country running for his life and before he can even take a big breath he's telling us how to run the show. The arrogance of the guy!' (p.44), and
- age – 3rd Juror generalises his difficult experiences with his own son into a prejudice against young people: 'It's the kids, the way they are nowadays. Angry! Hostile! You can't do a damn thing with them' (p.12), and later 'That goddamn rotten kid. I know him. What they're like. What they do to you. How they kill you every day' (p.59).

Specifics versus generalisations

Stereotypes use generalisations to characterise people, and 10th Juror is particularly prone to stereotyping the defendant based on socio-economic background. He regularly makes generalised statements about 'those people' (p.6), without ever justifying his opinions with concrete details. Examples include:

- 'I'm tellin' you they let the kids run wild up there' (p.6),
- '... you're not going to tell us that we're supposed to believe that kid, knowing what he is. Listen, I've lived among 'em all my life. You can't believe a word they say. I mean, they're born liars.' (p.8),
- 'The kids who crawl outa those places are real trash. I don't want any part of them, I'm telling you' (p.12),
- 'Let's talk facts. These people are born to lie' … 'I've known some who were OK, but that's the exception' (pp.51–2),
- 'They're violent, they're vicious, they're ignorant, and they will cut us up' (p.53).

The one instance where 10th Juror uses details is when he argues 'his type, they're multiplying five times as fast as we are. That's the statistic.' (p.53). Yet he only uses this statistic to ground his own fears: 'They're against us, they hate us, they want to destroy us ... if we don't smack them down whenever we can, then they are gonna own us. They're gonna breed us out of existence' (p.53).

10th Juror is not the only one guilty of such generalisation and stereotyping. For example, 4th states:

> This boy ... he's a product of a filthy neighbourhood and a broken home ... Slums are breeding grounds for criminals. I know it. So do you. It's no secret. Children from slum backgrounds are potential menaces to society. (p.12)

Similarly, 3rd Juror muses:

> ... sometimes I think we'd be better off if we took these tough kids and slapped 'em down before they make trouble, you know? Save us a lot of time and money. (p.3)

Neither 4th nor 3rd jurors make reference to specific details of the defendant's situation, but rather rely on generalised stereotypes which support their own prejudices against 'those people'.

In fact, 8th is the only juror to carefully review specific details from the case rather than resorting to general class stereotypes. He notes:

> ... this boy's been kicked around all his life. You know – living in a slum, his mother dead since he was nine. He spent a year and a half in an orphanage while his father served a jail term for forgery. (p.8)

This lists specific facts and variables about the boy's upbringing, rather than distilling him into a non-specific member of a socio-economic group. Similarly, in 8th Juror's speech on page 23, he lists specific details of the victim's rough existence – his gambling, his convictions, his employment history. This can be contrasted with 10th Juror's simplistic and prejudiced attitude: 'Listen, we know the father was a bum' (p.24).

The contrast between these two attitudes is that 8th Juror is attempting to form his opinions based on the specific factors affecting the defendant and the victim, and trying to focus on the human beings in the case at hand. 10th Juror is content to convict the defendant based on stereotypes and generalised tendencies of others in similar situations.

Once again, by aligning the less simplistic attitude with 8th Juror, *Twelve Angry Men* endorses compassion and condemns prejudice and stereotyping.

Challenging stereotypes

The play doesn't offer a great deal of hope about resisting and challenging prejudice, though on several occasions jurors try to point out the risks of resorting to familiar and comforting stereotypes and generalisations. For example, 8th Juror questions why 10th is convinced by the testimony of the second witness, even though she is part of the same socio-economic environment as the defendant: 'You don't believe the boy. How come you believe the woman? She's one of "them", too, isn't she?' (p.10). Another example is when 5th Juror points out that he comes from the same background as the defendant, but that his life hasn't necessarily turned out the way that the stereotypes would predict: 'I've lived in a slum all my life. I nurse that trash in Harlem Hospital six nights a week ... I used to play in a backyard that was filled with garbage. Maybe it still smells on me' (p.12). Through moments like this, Rose challenges us to rethink our prejudices and to recognise the risks of generalisation.

Q What evidence is there in the text to show how 10th Juror and others have formed their stereotypes?

Decisions

Key quotes

'I urge you to deliberate honestly and thoughtfully ... I don't envy you your job.' (p.1)

'It's not easy for me to raise my hand and send a boy off to die without talking about it first.' (p.7)

'You couldn't change my mind if you talked for a hundred years.' (p.7, 7th Juror – the fifth to change his mind)

'Five of them already have changed their minds. There's no reason why they can't be persuaded to do it again.' (p.42)

Not only must each individual juror come to their own decision about whether or not the defendant is guilty, but the group together must reach a unanimous decision in order to deliver a verdict.

Twelve Angry Men charts the decision-making process, and we see how each juror's decision is influenced by facts, evidence, discussion and personal belief. These factors – whether fairly or unfairly – inform and influence their decisions and ultimately their collective verdict regarding the defendant. In weighing up the case, the jurors have a range of information at their disposal, which can be grouped into a number of areas.

Personal qualities of the defendant

These include the boy's background, his age, his character, his criminal history and, for many of the jurors, generalised stereotypes based on his socio-economic identity or on unsubstantiated facts about his character. Jurors mention the following personal qualities in their discussions:

- He's a killer by nature: 'The man's a dangerous killer. You could see it.' (p.7),
- He's a liar: 'You can't believe a word they say ... they're born liars.' (p.8),
- His memory is unreliable: '... the boy's entire story was flimsy. He claimed he was at the movies ... and yet ... couldn't remember what films he saw or who played in them.' (p.10),
- He is a known criminal: 'Look at his record.' (p.11),
- He's angry: he has been regularly beaten by his father and that is 'a motive for him to be an angry kid' (p.11),
- Like other youth, he's inclined to poor behaviour: 'It's the kids, the way they are nowadays.' (p.12),
- He's destined, by virtue of his upbringing, to crime: 'Children from slum backgrounds are potential menaces to society.' (p.12),
- He had a motive: 'The boy had a motive ... the beatings and all.' (p.23),
- He's smarter than they're giving him credit for: '... do you really think the boy would shout out a thing like that ... ? I don't think so. He's much too bright for that.' (p.28), and
- He's a potential murderer: the court psychologist said he was a 'killer-type' (p.46)

Key point

11th Juror makes an important point about the difference between possibility and probability: the fact that the defendant's psychological profile revealed 'strong homicidal tendencies' (p.46) does not provide evidence that he would necessarily have acted on these potentials. As he notes, 'we should remember that many of us are capable of committing murder. But few of us do' (p.47).

The strength of the prosecution's case (including the prosecutor, witnesses, and argument)

These factors include the information jurors relate from the courtroom, reminding us how compelling the jurors find the 'facts' of the case:

- 'I thought he was really sharp. I mean, the way he hammered home his points, one by one, in logical sequence. It takes a good brain to do that. I was very impressed' (p.5),
- A witness '... heard the kid shout out, "I'm gonna kill you"' (p.9),
- 'You can't refute facts' (p.10),
- 'What about that woman across the street? If her testimony doesn't prove it, nothing does' (p.10), and
- '... that testimony from those people across the hall ... that was very powerful' (p.11).

On the other hand, 8th Juror concentrates on the failings of the defence lawyer when he explains some of the reasons he still feels reasonable doubt about the guilt of the defendant:

- '... I started to feel that the defence counsel wasn't doing his job. He let too many things go' (p.13),
- 'I would have asked for another lawyer ... I'd want my lawyer to tear the prosecution witnesses to shreds, or at least to try' (p.14), and
- 'The lawyer was court-appointed ... It could mean he didn't want the case. It could mean he resented being appointed' (p.29).

Personal feelings and intuition

The third broad group of factors influencing juror decisions is less tangible. Many of the jurors cite 'feelings' about the case – intuitions probably based on factors like those above (personal characteristics or persuasiveness of legal argument) that jurors are sometimes unable to articulate definitively. Instead, they make statements such as:

- '... it's hard to put into words. I just – think he's guilty' (p.9), or
- '... I started to get a peculiar feeling about this trial' (p.13).

Although 3rd Juror claims early on that he has 'no personal feelings about this' (p.9), he eventually admits 'I'm a very excitable person, y'know' and 'I get moved by this' (p.42), suggesting that his personal feelings *are* contributing to his decision.

Rose highlights the complex interplay of factors contributing to individual decision-making processes, reminding us that the powerful and formalised legal system is, at heart, dependent on individual human beings and their complex psychological motivations.

Q Does *Twelve Angry Men* privilege any one group of decision-making factors over the others, or suggest that any particular variables are more valid than others?

Doubt and certainty

Key quotes

'He doesn't say the boy is not guilty. He just isn't sure.' (p.20)

'He's guilty for sure. There's not a doubt in the whole world.' (p.22)

'What reasonable doubt? That's nothing but words.' (p.32)

'... we have a reasonable doubt, and this is a safeguard which has enormous value in our system. No jury can declare a man guilty unless it's sure. We nine can't understand how you three are still so sure.' (p.53)

Rose spends a significant portion of the play investigating the notion of 'reasonable doubt', the clause in the legal system which demands that jurors be certain of a defendant's guilt.

Each of the jurors has a different degree of certainty about the opinions they hold, with corresponding levels of confidence about fighting for those opinions. Certainty, in this context, is a kind of faith: it is not necessarily dependent on concrete evidence, as the play indicates that very few facts can be absolute. Instead, individuals must make up their minds based on the apparent likelihood of various events and on their own personal beliefs.

8th Juror argues most strongly throughout the play for the impossibility of certainty. He regularly reminds the others that 'The burden of proof is on the prosecution' (p.9) and that their task is merely to decide whether or not the defendant's guilt is beyond doubt. To return a verdict of 'not guilty', the jurors do not need to reach certainty about the defendant's innocence, they must merely admit that they have doubt about his guilt as argued by the prosecution. When viewed from this perspective, it is easy to see why 8th is able to eventually change the minds of the eleven other jurors. By proposing a series of alternative possible (even though, by his own admission, not very probable) explanations for various details of the case, he is able to challenge the others' certainty. Rose's play shows that when it is difficult to maintain certainty about one's beliefs, doubt is a reasonable and intelligent state of mind.

Q Does *Twelve Angry Men* provide any examples of certainty winning out over doubt?

DIFFERENT INTERPRETATIONS

Different interpretations arise from different responses to a text. These responses can be published in newspapers, journals and books by critics and reviewers, or they can be expressed in discussions among readers in the media, classrooms, book groups and so on. Productions of stage plays, or screen adaptations of stage plays, are also interpretations of the text (the script). While there is no single correct reading or interpretation of a text, it is important to understand that an interpretation is more than an 'opinion' – it is the justification of a point of view on the text. To present an interpretation of the text based on your point of view you must use a logical argument and support it with relevant evidence from the text.

Productions and reviews

Although it is difficult to locate records of the reception of the original telemovie, or indeed early productions of the stage play, there are some surviving responses to the 1957 film. This gives some indication of how Rose's teleplay was probably received, and it seems likely that these responses echo the reception of the stage play too. Responses to the 1957 film appear to have been largely favourable, commending Rose's ability to explore important social issues and domestic conflict in a theatrically engaging forum. Eleanor Roosevelt was keen to praise the film when she saw it, saying that 'it makes vivid what reasonable doubt means when a murder trial jury makes up its mind on circumstantial evidence' (Thomas 1983, p.157). Despite such responses, however, the film was not a commercial hit.

Reviews of more recent productions show that while stylistically the script may have dated, its content stands the test of time and it can still provide the basis for powerful and moving stage productions. Peter Marks, for example, in his review of the Roundabout Theatre Company's 2006 production, admits that the play might not be 'the subtlest piece of writing' but that there is something 'theatrically irresistible' about 'the idea of twelve men of wildly different temperaments and views being forced to coexist until they have reached a consensus' (Marks 2006). Similarly, reviews of a production directed by playwright Harold Pinter in 1996 argue that although the play is a product of its time, it still presents an engaging argument about the workings of the American judicial system and the power of individuals to affect others' lives and fates.

Film and television interpretations

The 'interpretations' provided by both the 1957 film version and the 1997 telemovie version of *Twelve Angry Men* are remarkably consistent with each other. Rose is credited as the screenwriter for both, and although they had two different directors and were produced four decades apart, both reproduce the dialogue, concerns and themes of the play quite faithfully.

Aside from minor alterations of lines (and, especially in the 1997 production, the modernising of some social and sporting allusions), both the film and the telemovie follow the script almost slavishly. Just like the stage play they take place within the jury room (with the exception of opening and closing shots either in the court room or the court house, setting the scene). They do not employ sophisticated editing, sound-effects or other techniques, but rather present the drama very much as though it were taking place on a naturalistic stage.

Several moments in each production deviate from the stage play, serving to shift interpretations slightly or highlight particular elements or themes. These include:

- the omission of a discussion about motive (on page 23 of the stage script): this shifts focus at this point to the discussion of reasonable doubt (1957 film),
- the close-up of a photograph of 3rd Juror's son in the final moments, emphasising the personal connection he has made to the defendant (1957 film),
- explicit references to race (with several African American jurors and occasional discussion of the impact of race relations on the jury's deliberations) and to religion (with 10th Juror identifying himself as formerly of Islamic faith) (1997 telemovie), and
- the omission of 8th Juror's speech about prejudice and the judicial system (page 53 of the stage version), making 8th seem less didactic but also less passionate.

Two possible interpretations

The following two interpretations demonstrate how the same text can be read as support for two contrasting views, as long as direct evidence from the text is used to build the arguments.

Reading 1

***Twelve Angry Men* critiques a judicial system that is inherently susceptible to individual human bias and error, and is therefore flawed.**

Reginald Rose constructs his play in such a way that the audience can never be certain of the defendant's guilt or innocence; the jurors themselves are never certain, and we are not privy to any knowledge beyond what they know. Since we are uncertain, we are confronted with the fact that a jury can only ever convict or acquit based on the information available to them, on their own biases and backgrounds and on their own deliberations on the matter. 8th Juror, discussing the implications of court-appointed lawyers, even points out that not only jurors but lawyers themselves are subject to bias (p.29).

The unrelenting arguments between the twelve jurors remind us that legal cases are rarely straightforward, that even when a jury is almost unanimous (as at the beginning of the play), minds may still be changed. As the stage direction on page 22 reveals, 8th Juror '*does not know, and never will*' know whether he is responsible for letting a guilty man walk free. All he can do is trust his own instincts, and in the end these instincts are responsible for the reversal of the eleven other jurors' decisions, the verdict handed down on the defendant and ultimately the impact this will have on the defendant's immediate and wider community.

At the beginning of the play, the jurors are nearly unanimous in their willingness to convict the defendant, based on what they have seen in court and on what they each believe about the defendant. As 8th Juror progressively demonstrates, the evidence presented in court (including witness testimonies and exhibits such as the supposedly unique switch-knife) is not always as watertight as it first seems. His arguments offer the other jurors good grounds to reasonably doubt the defendant's guilt. However, this does not give the audience faith in the system: instead, we are left to wonder how 'facts' or truths can ever really be established, when a single jury member can so successfully derail a prosecution's case. The implication is that 8th Juror's arguments could be equally flawed, and the jury's decision could well result in the 'return' of 'a guilty man to the community' (p.53). Further, there is the suggestion that each juror's subjective emotional connection to the case can impair his judgement.

The play doesn't argue that the judicial system is biased in any particular direction, but that it can make mistakes in favour of either guilt or innocence. The 'not guilty' verdict in this particular case could easily be wrong, but in other cases 'It's happened before that someone's been convicted of murder and executed, and years later someone else has confessed to the crime' (p.29). We are left with the overwhelming feeling that the responsibility on individuals and juries is great, given that the absolute truth of any crime can rarely be known for certain.

Reading 2

***Twelve Angry Men* extols the virtues of a judicial system based on compassionate, reasoned decisions made by ordinary people.**

The play is an examination of the protracted deliberations of a jury, and thus an argument for the values of a system which allows individuals to discuss, debate and decide a case based on the information presented to them in court. As 3rd Juror says, 'Everybody deserves a fair trial. That's the system' (p.3).

At the beginning of the play, eleven of the twelve jurors are ready to convict the defendant, even though much of the evidence they have heard in the court case is indirect or 'circumstantial' (p.14). However, 8th Juror argues that the notion of a fair trial involves not just fair access to legal representation in the court, but that they should not 'send a boy off to die without talking about it first' (p.7); the members of the jury hold the power of life and death in their hands and they must use that power wisely.

Later, 11th Juror further articulates this notion when he praises the judicial system as a symbol of democracy. He is proud of his role in a society in which jurors are 'notified by mail to come down to this place and decide on the guilt or innocence of a man we have never heard of before', and he goes on to remind the other jurors that they 'have nothing to gain or lose by this verdict. This is one of the reasons we are strong' (p.39). Rose's play argues that this democratic system of judgement empowers not only individual members of society (whether jurors or the accused), but society itself, in respecting the intelligence, fairness and compassion of its members and endowing them with power over each others' fates.

Even though we never learn whether or not the defendant committed the crime, 8th Juror's arguments demonstrate that there is reasonable doubt about the defendant's guilt, and that to condemn him to death would therefore be an immoral decision. The play suggests that rational discussion can overcome initial prejudiced responses to a case, and therefore that the judicial system is moral and valuable.

QUESTIONS & ANSWERS

This section focuses on your own analytical writing on the text, and gives you strategies for producing high-quality responses in your coursework and exam essays.

Essay writing – an overview

An essay is a formal and serious piece of writing that presents your point of view on the text, usually in response to a given essay topic. Your 'point of view' in an essay is your interpretation of the meaning of the text's language, structure, characters, situations and events, supported by detailed analysis of textual evidence.

Analyse – don't summarise

In your essays it is important to avoid simply summarising what happens in a text:

- A **summary** is a description or paraphrase (retelling in different words) of the characters and events. For example: 'Macbeth has a horrifying vision of a dagger dripping with blood before he goes to murder King Duncan'.
- An **analysis** is an explanation of the real meaning or significance that lies 'beneath' the text's words (and images, for a film). For example: 'Macbeth's vision of a bloody dagger shows how deeply uneasy he is

about the violent act he is contemplating – as well as his sense that supernatural forces are impelling him to act'.

A limited amount of summary is sometimes necessary to let your reader know which part of the text you wish to discuss. However, always keep this to a minimum and follow it immediately with your analysis (explanation) of what this part of the text is really telling us.

Plan your essay

Carefully plan your essay so that you have a clear idea of what you are going to say. The plan ensures that your ideas flow logically, that your argument remains consistent and that you stay on the topic. An essay plan should be a list of **brief dot points** – no more than half a page. It includes:

- your central argument or main contention – a concise statement (usually in a single sentence) of your overall response to the topic. See 'Analysing a sample topic' for guidelines on how to formulate a main contention.
- three or four dot points for each paragraph indicating the main idea and evidence/examples from the text. Note that in your essay you will need to *expand* on these points and *analyse* the evidence.

Structure your essay

An essay is a complete, self-contained piece of writing. It has a clear beginning (the introduction), middle (several body paragraphs) and end (the last paragraph or conclusion). It must also have a central argument that runs throughout, linking each paragraph to form a coherent whole.

See examples of introductions and conclusions in the 'Analysing a sample topic' and 'Sample answer' sections.

The introduction establishes your overall response to the topic. It includes your main contention and outlines the main evidence you will refer to in the course of the essay. Write your introduction *after* you have done a plan and *before* you write the rest of the essay.

The body paragraphs argue your case – they present evidence from the text and explain how this evidence supports your argument. Each body paragraph needs:

- a strong **topic sentence** (usually the first sentence) that states the main point being made in the paragraph
- **evidence** from the text, including some brief quotations
- **analysis** of the textual evidence explaining its significance and **explanation** of how it supports your argument
- **links back to the topic** in one or more statements, usually towards the end of the paragraph.

Connect the body paragraphs so that your discussion flows smoothly. Use some linking words and phrases like 'similarly' and 'on the other hand', though don't start every paragraph like this. Another strategy is to use a significant word from the last sentence of one paragraph in the first sentence of the next.

Use key terms from the topic – or synonyms for them – throughout, so the relevance of your discussion to the topic is always clear.

The conclusion ties everything together and finishes the essay. It includes strong statements that emphasise your central argument and provide a clear response to the topic.

Avoid simply restating the points made earlier in the essay – this will end on a very flat note and imply that you have run out of ideas and vocabulary. The conclusion is meant to be a logical extension of what you have written, not just a repetition or summary of it. Writing an effective conclusion can be a challenge. Try using these tips:

- Start by linking back to the final sentence of the second-last paragraph rather than just leaping to your main contention straight away. This helps your writing to 'flow'.
- Use synonyms and expressions with equivalent meanings to vary your vocabulary. This allows you to reinforce your line of argument without being repetitive.

- When planning your essay, think of one or two broad statements or observations about the text's wider meaning. These should be related to the topic and your overall argument. Keep them for the conclusion, since they will give you something 'new' to say but still follow logically from your discussion. The introduction will be focused on the topic, but the conclusion can present a wider view of the text.

Essay topics

1 'The relationship between 3rd and 8th jurors is the most important element in *Twelve Angry Men*.' Discuss.

2 3rd Juror says that 'everybody deserves a fair trial'. Does the defendant in this case get a fair trial?

3 '*Twelve Angry Men* shows that personal experience is the strongest factor influencing human decision-making processes.' Discuss.

4 'In *Twelve Angry Men*, the characteristics of gentleness and rationality are valued above all else.' Discuss.

5 '8th Juror has no character flaws, just as 3rd Juror has no redeeming features.' Discuss.

6 10th Juror says 'what you want to believe, you believe'. How does *Twelve Angry Men* show that we believe what we want to believe?

7 *Twelve Angry Men* takes place in 'real time'. How does Rose use this structure to strengthen his examination of the judicial system?

8 '*Twelve Angry Men* is a play about the impossibility of certainty.' Discuss.

9 10th Juror is very passionate about the defendant's guilt. How convincing is the moment when he changes his mind?

10 '*Twelve Angry Men* presents the pessimistic opinion that all humans are fallible.' Do you agree?

Vocabulary for writing on *Twelve Angry Men*

Foil: A foil is a character who provides a contrast to another character (usually the main protagonist) by exhibiting differences in personality, beliefs, behaviours and other qualities. Sometimes a character might serve as a foil in just one scene or dialogue. In this play, 3rd Juror is a foil for 8th throughout the whole work, and serves to highlight the unique aspects of 8th's character that allow him to stand alone against the jury and ultimately change all their minds.

Denouement: The events in a play or literary work that follow the final climax and provide the resolution or conclusion of the work.

Foreshadowing: A technique whereby the author plants incidents, actions or dialogue which hint at and, to an extent, allow audiences to predict (or at least partially expect) later important events.

Analysing a sample topic

'The relationship between 3rd and 8th jurors is the most important element in *Twelve Angry Men*.' Discuss.

You might begin by making a list of important quotes and incidents for each of the two characters (examples are listed in the 'Characters & Relationships' section), and important moments between them. This will help you support your argument once you start writing.

The second part of the question asks you to identify the most important aspect of the play. To address this, it would be useful to list other main elements in *Twelve Angry Men*, such as:

- the notion of reasonable doubt
- attitudes of prejudice
- conflicts between jurors.

You then need to form a contention – your response to the question asked by the topic. Usually you will need to argue *for* or *against* the topic, and explain why. In this case, by making the list above, you can see that 3rd and 8th jurors' relationship actually illustrates all the other important issues. So your contention, or central argument, might be, '3rd and 8th jurors' relationship is the most important element in the play because it illustrates the other central issues and themes'.

Sample introduction

> There are many elements of *Twelve Angry Men* that serve to address the text's themes of decision-making and legal justice. Reginald Rose uses these various elements to challenge his audience to consider issues such as what influences our decisions and whether the justice system is fair and ethical. Such elements include not only themes and ideas like prejudice or the validity of witness testimony, but also more concrete aspects of the play like the main characters or the shifting dynamics between the jurors. While several elements (including reasonable doubt, prejudice and jury-room conflict) can be identified as central, the most important of these is the relationship between 3rd and 8th jurors. The development of this relationship drives and shapes the action of the play, and it can be seen to encompass and illustrate all of Rose's other central themes.

Body paragraph outline

Paragraph 1 – introduce 8th and 3rd jurors' relationship, explaining why it is a central element of the play:

- Briefly describe the two characters individually before discussing their relationship.
- Summarise the nature of the relationship, including the characters' similarities, differences and specific interactions, such as the physical incidents on pages 37, 48 and 59.
- Explain how the relationship fits into the play as a whole – for example, the three incidents above represent important points of climax and resolution in the shape of the narrative.
- Note briefly that aspects of the relationship comment upon other important themes and ideas in the play.

Paragraph 2 – contextualise this relationship beside other important elements of the play (particularly those mentioned in the introduction):

- Discuss the notion of reasonable doubt – explain what it means, reference discussions from the text (e.g. 8th Juror's speech, p.53).

- Discuss attitudes of prejudice, using examples (e.g. 10th Juror's speech pp.52–3).
- Discuss the jury-room conflicts using direct evidence from text, including disagreements over the case and personal conflicts.

Paragraph 3 – explain how this relationship illustrates all other important elements of the play:

- 8th Juror is the character who most clearly understands 'reasonable doubt' and 3rd is the least willing to accept it – the clashes in their relationship represent the struggle to come to terms with the concept of reasonable doubt.
- Show how 3rd and 8th jurors represent extremes: 3rd tends towards stereotyping and prejudice, while 8th is more balanced, and their relationship embodies the effects of prejudice on decisions and interactions.
- Reference specific instances of conflict between 3rd and 8th jurors (such as the disagreement about what's 'possible', p.16), explain how these are primary examples of conflicts that arise in jury-room situations.

Sample conclusion

> While there are multiple elements that can be seen as central in this play, the relationship between 3rd and 8th jurors is clearly the most important of these. Their relationship not only exemplifies Rose's central study of decision-making in a judicial context, but symbolically represents the progression of the play. From the opening moments when they oppose each other in their opinions on the case, through the incidents of physical conflict between them, to the play's conclusion when 3rd has accepted 8th's perspective and accepts his help to put on his coat, the shifts in this relationship reflect the play's larger narrative shifts. The dynamics of the relationship symbolise the conflicts within the room, and through these characters Rose also challenges audience members to confront their own beliefs and prejudices.

SAMPLE ANSWER

'*Twelve Angry Men* presents the pessimistic view that all humans are flawed.' Discuss.

In *Twelve Angry Men*, Reginald Rose consistently demonstrates that humans are flawed creatures – from the twelve jurors to the prosecution's witnesses to the defendant himself, people are constantly revealing their weaknesses and imperfections. No characters in the play are faultless, and their various flaws underpin the actions and conflicts in the jury-room as well as the details of the murder case which form the narrative's basis. However, the play does not argue that human flaws are always cause for despair; rather, it advocates accepting the realities of our flaws so that we may carry on with our lives in the best way that we can.

The scope of human imperfection presented in the play is, indeed, extensive. The trial itself paints a bleak portrait of humanity: the crime in question is first degree murder – one of the ugliest imaginable acts one human can commit against another. Here, even the victim is not portrayed as innocent, but as a 'tough, cruel, primitive kind of man' – guilty of gambling and fighting, among other wrongs. The lawyers on the case, too, are described variously as 'just plain stupid', not doing their jobs thoroughly enough or lacking motivation to win the case.

Many other human flaws are identified in discussions of both defendant and witness testimonies. One example is inaccuracy of memory: the defendant weakens his own alibi because he cannot recall details of a film he claims to have seen. Another example of flawed behaviour is the second witness's vanity, which results in potentially deceptive testimony: in court she tries to appear younger than she is, and her 'eyesight' (and therefore testimony) 'is in question' by the end of the play.

It is not just offstage characters who are shown to be imperfect. Each juror has deficiencies and less-than-ideal qualities, whether these emerge through their interactions with each other or their attitudes towards the trial. For example, 10th Juror is prejudiced, regularly using stereotypes to condemn the defendant without stopping to consider whether the boy really *is* a 'very big drinker' or a 'born liar'. Similarly, 3rd Juror is guilty of stereotyping the defendant based on age, and he defends his opinions and stereotypes violently in the jury-room, such as his near-attack on 8th Juror at the end of the first act. The play does not let a single character escape unflawed. Even 8th Juror, constructed as a gentle, admirable character and one with whom we should empathise, is not perfect. He himself admits that he 'broke the law' buying the switch-knife in order to make his point about reasonable doubt.

'Flaws' are not just clear-cut behaviours like prejudice, violence or crime. In many cases, characters' fallibilities are the result of qualities that are, of themselves, not necessarily considered negative. For example, in the jury-room discussions, when 8th Juror discredits the testimony of the first witness, he doesn't accuse the witness of lying. Instead, other jurors argue that he is a 'frightened, insignificant old man who has been nothing all his life', and perhaps these factors led him to unconsciously convince himself of his own testimony. His inaccurate testimony is not the result of intentional or malicious behaviour, but simply of basic human fallibility. The jurors, therefore, do not hold a grudge against him, nor does the play suggest that such flaws are evidence of a hopeless world. Instead we are reminded that behaviour is always complex and influenced by many variables, and that we should simply be aware of this.

The play examines flaws (whether of character, behaviour or ability) as innate human qualities. But this fact is not presented in a pessimistic way – human imperfection is never portrayed as evidence that there are no positives. Rather, flaws are portrayed as basic facts of life. They may actually have their benefits, as we see from 8th Juror's speech reminding us that while prejudices interfere with truth, no 'real damage has been done here'. He argues that even the apparently flawed state of doubt can be a *positive*: a 'safeguard' against unfair convictions. He is optimistic that the jurors have made the best decision they can, under the circumstances. This is supported by his gentle gestures of compassion towards 3rd Juror at the end of the play, as he helps him with his jacket. Rose is careful to leave us with this optimistic image as the final commentary from the play, ensuring that we do not see human flaws in a pessimistic way.

Even 3rd Juror, who holds such a pessimistic view of young people, is forced to change his vote by the end of the play, and to conclude that despite his flaws, the defendant may not be guilty. While the play paints a striking picture of a deeply flawed society, Rose does not encourage us to feel pessimistic about this. His central character, 8th Juror, is never worn down by others' (or his own) faults, but instead works hard to consider all reasonable possibilities and give his fellow humans the benefit of the doubt. *Twelve Angry Men* ultimately leaves its audience feeling hopeful about a flawed world.

REFERENCES & READING

Text

Rose, Reginald 1977, *Twelve Angry Men*, Samuel French, London.

DVD

12 Angry Men 1957, dir. Sydney Lumet, Orion-Nova. Starring Henry Fonda and Lee J. Cobb.

12 Angry Men 1997, dir. William Friedkin, Metro-Goldwyn-Mayer. Starring Jack Lemmon and George C. Scott.

Websites

Duhaime, Lloyd 2010, *Duhaime.org*, http://www.duhaime.org/

A site with accessible dictionaries of legal terminology; obviously only to be relied upon for help understanding this text, not as binding legal information or advice!

IMDb.com 2010, *The Internet Movie Database*, http://www.imdb.com/

Marks, Peter 2006, '*Twelve Angry Men* Returns With Conviction', Washington Post, http://www.washingtonpost.com/wp-dyn/content/article/2006/10/05/AR2006100501855.html

Pinter, Harold 2003 'Directing: Twelve Angry Men', http://www.haroldpinter.org/directing/directing_angry.shtml

Harold Pinter website containing extracts from reviews of his 1996 production.

Other references

Bigsby, C.W.E. 1992, *Modern American Drama: 1945–1990*, Cambridge University Press, Cambridge.

Downer, Alan 1961, *Recent American Drama: No 7 University of Minnesota Pamphlets on American Writers*, University of Minnesota, Minneapolis.

Loftus, Elizabeth 1996, *Eyewitness Testimony*, Harvard University Press, Cambridge (first published 1979).

Thomas, Tony 1983, *The Complete Films of Henry Fonda*, Citadel Press, NJ.